Evidence-Based Policy

More advance praise for *Evidence-Based Policy*

"Using evidence to inform public policy seems like the natural, smart, and effective thing to do. But acting on this intuition can be fraught with complexity and can lead to decisions that are neither smart nor effective. Evidence-Based Policy is the primer we have been waiting for, and with its marvelous blend of theory and examples provides compelling evidence that improved decision making is possible."

—Michael Feuer, *Dean of the Graduate School of Education and Human Development at The George Washington University, and author of Moderating the Debate: Rationality and the Promise of American Education*

"Evidence-based policy is in the doldrums—lost between over-simplistic technical approaches for judging the effectiveness of interventions and over-cynical assertions that politics conquers all. Cartwright and Hardie have produced a much needed fillip in this admirably clear and immensely practical guide. They show how decision support is a matter of using both data and discretion. It is an outstanding contribution that will be of great value to beginners and experienced practitioners alike."

—Ray Pawson, *author of Evidence-based Policy: A Realist Perspective and co-author of Realistic Evaluation*

"Chock full of accessible examples, this book explains clearly and cogently what's involved in making intelligent use of evidence in developing social policy. It should be essential reading for all wanting to contribute to effective evidence-based policy."

—Nick Tilley, *author of Crime Prevention and co-author of Realistic Evaluation*

"This well-written book reflects many of the central ideas that underlie my Reports on Child Protection in England. It combines rigorous theory with a valuable profusion of tips and case studies to give practical advice on how to think about what evidence you really need."

—Eileen Munro, *author of the U.K. Government commissioned 2011 independent review of child protection in England*

Evidence-Based Policy
A Practical Guide to Doing It Better

Nancy Cartwright and Jeremy Hardie

OXFORD
UNIVERSITY PRESS

OXFORD
UNIVERSITY PRESS

Oxford University Press is a department of the University of Oxford.
It furthers the University's objective of excellence in research,
scholarship, and education by publishing worldwide.

Oxford   New York
Auckland   Cape Town   Dar es Salaam   Hong Kong   Karachi
Kuala Lumpur   Madrid   Melbourne   Mexico City   Nairobi
New Delhi   Shanghai   Taipei   Toronto

With offices in
Argentina   Austria   Brazil   Chile   Czech Republic   France   Greece
Guatemala   Hungary   Italy   Japan   Poland   Portugal   Singapore
South Korea   Switzerland   Thailand   Turkey   Ukraine   Vietnam

Oxford is a registered trade mark of Oxford University Press in the UK and certain other countries.

Published in the United States of America by Oxford University Press
198 Madison Avenue, New York, NY 10016

© Oxford University Press 2012

Library of Congress Cataloging-in-Publication Data
Cartwright, Nancy.
Evidence-based policy : a practical guide to doing it better / Nancy Cartwright and Jeremy Hardie.
p.   cm.
Includes bibliographical references and index.
ISBN 978-0-19-984162-2 (pbk. : alk. paper) — ISBN 978-0-19-984160-8 (hbk. : alk. paper)
1. Policy sciences. 2. Policy sciences—Evaluation. 3. Human services—Planning.
4. Human services—Evaluation. I. Hardie, Jeremy. II. Title.
H97.C375   2012
320.6—dc23   2012022991

CONTENTS

Acknowledgments   *vii*

PREFACE: Do You Want to Read This Book?
Putting Our Conclusions First   *ix*

PART ONE: Getting Started: From "It Worked There"
to "It Will Work Here"
I.A: What's in This Book and Why   *3*
I.B: The Theory That Backs Up What We Say   *14*

PART TWO: Paving the Road from "There" to "Here"
II.A: Support Factors: Causal Cakes and Their Ingredients   *61*
II.B: Causal Roles: Shared and Unshared   *76*

PART THREE: Strategies for Finding What You Need to Know
III.A: Where We Are and Where We Are Going   *91*
III.B: Four Strategies   *94*

PART FOUR: RCTs, Evidence-Ranking Schemes, and Fidelity
IV.A: Where We Are and Where We Are Going   *121*
IV.B: What Are RCTs Good For?   *122*
IV.C: Evidence-Ranking Schemes, Advice Guides,
    and Choosing Effective Policies   *135*
IV.D: Fidelity   *144*

PART FIVE: Deliberation Is Not Second Best
V.A: Where We Are and Where We Are Going   *157*
V.B: Centralization and Discretion   *160*

CONCLUSION   *172*

Appendix I: Representing Causal Processes   175
Appendix II: The Munro Review   179
Appendix III: CCTV and Car Theft   181
Notes   187
References   191
Index   195

ACKNOWLEDGMENTS

Nancy and Jeremy would like to thank the following for their contributions to this project: Margaret Atwood, Tracey Brown, Emily Cartwright, Angus Deaton, Luke Dowdney, Damien Fennell, Charles Gee, Gerd Gigerenzer, Charlotte Hardie, Mike Hough, Jeremy Howick, Sandra Jay, John Kay, Andrew Kelly, John Krebs, Eric Martin, Eleonora Montuschi, Eileen Munro, Alex de Pledge, Nicola Pollock, Kenneth Prewitt, Julian Reiss, Jane Roberts, Rebecca Robinson, Ben Rogers, Alice Sampson, Hakan Seckinelgin, Nicola Singleton, Adam Spray, Jacob Stegenga, Kirsteen Tait, David Tuckett, David Wiggins, Michael Feuer, and the members of the LSE Evidence for Use project. We are also grateful to Alex Marcellesi for efficient, effective, and informed editing.

Nancy Cartwright's work on this book was supported over the past several years by a British Academy Research Development Award, "A Theory of Evidence for Use"; an Arts and Humanities Research Council research grant, "Choices of Evidence: Tacit Philosophical Assumptions in the Debates within the Campbell Collaboration"; a John Templeton Foundation grant, "God's Order, Man's Order and the Order of Nature"; a Spencer Foundation grant, "Evidence for Use: Prolegomena to a Theory of Evidence-Based Education Policy"; and by the LSE's Grantham Research Institute on Climate Change and the Environment. She would like to thank all of these for their help.

PREFACE: DO YOU WANT TO READ THIS BOOK? PUTTING OUR CONCLUSIONS FIRST

Evidence-based policy. You are told: use policies that work. And you are told: RCTs—randomized controlled trials—will show you what these are. That's not so. RCTs are great, but they do not do that for you. They cannot alone support the expectation that a policy will work for you. What they tell you is true—that this policy produced that result there. But they do not tell you why that is relevant to what you need to bet on getting the result you want here. For that, you will need to know a lot more. That's what this book is about. We are going to show what else you have to have and how you set about finding it.

We put these conclusions at the start because you should not bother with this book unless you are able to accept them. We do not, of course, mean that you have to accept them now. But you must be open to accepting them if our arguments are good.

Like us, you want evidence that a policy will work here, where you are. Randomized controlled trials do not tell you that. They do not even tell you that a policy works. What they tell you is that a policy worked there, where the trial was carried out, in that population. Our argument is that the changes in tense—from "worked" to "work" to "will work"—are not just a matter of grammatical detail. To move from one to the other requires hard intellectual and practical effort. The fact that it worked there is indeed fact. But for that fact to be evidence that it will work here, it needs to be relevant to that conclusion. To make RCTs relevant you need a lot more information and of a very different kind. What kind? That's what this book is about.

Evidence-Based Policy

PART ONE

Getting Started: From "It Worked There" to "It Will Work Here"

CHAPTER I.A

cℋ⌁

What's in This Book and Why

I.A.1 TWO CASES WHERE POLICIES WITH "GOOD EVIDENCE" WENT WRONG

I.A.1.1 The Bangladesh Integrated Nutrition Project

The World Bank estimates that in developing countries, 178 million children under 5 are stunted in growth and 55 million are underweight for their height. Malnutrition leaves children vulnerable to severe illness and death and has long-term consequences for the health of survivors. The World Bank has funded a wide range of nutritional interventions in developing countries in Latin America, the Caribbean, Africa, and East and South Asia. This included the Bangladesh Integrated Nutrition Project (BINP), modeled on its acclaimed predecessor, the Tamil Nadu Integrated Nutrition Project (TINP).[1] What was integrated? Feeding, health measures, and, centrally, education of pregnant mothers about how better to nourish their children and themselves to improve the health of their babies.

TINP covered the rural areas of districts with the worst nutritional status, about half the Tamil Nadu state, with a rural population of about 9 million. Malnutrition fell at a significant rate. The World Bank Independent Evaluation Group (1995) concluded that half to three fourths of the decline in TINP areas was due to TINP and other nutrition programs in those areas.

The Bangladesh Project was modeled on TINP. But Bangladesh's project had little success. A Save the Children UK (STC 2003) assessment concludes that program areas and nonprogram areas still had the same prevalence of malnutrition after six years and this despite the fact that the targeted health educational lessons sank in: carers in the BINP areas had on the whole greater knowledge about the caring practices advocated than those in non-BINP areas.

I.A.1.2 The California Class-Size Reduction Program

In the mid-1990s, California had evident problems with the academic achievement of its school pupils in the early grades of its public school system. For example, its fourth graders tied for last position among 39 states in the 1994 National Assessment of Education Progress.

For those thinking about what to do, the policy of reducing class sizes was salient. It fitted with popular opinion. Everyone—parents, teachers, politicians, educationalists—liked it as an idea and indeed continue to like it nearly 20 years later. And there was a commonsense view (meaning plausible because apparently congruent with a popularly accepted causal model, theory, or story about how children learn) that relied on notions such as that children benefit from closer attention from the teacher, that children are not all the same and the more special attention the better, and that these factors are particularly important if you are thinking about disadvantaged pupils.

But more was needed to validate commitment to a policy that turned out to be implemented statewide at a cost of $1 billion, rising to $1.6 billion, per annum. And there was more. The most important and compelling evidence came from the STAR project in Tennessee, from 1985, which was designed to be evaluated using a randomized controlled trial (RCT) research design. That evaluation concluded, inter alia, that students in the smaller classes performed better at all K-3 grade levels than did students in the larger classes. It also concluded that minority and inner-city children gained two or three times as much from reduced class sizes as did their white and nonurban peers. It thus confirmed an earlier meta-analysis that suggested, on the basis of studies that were not so rigorously designed, that large advantages can be expected to occur when class size is reduced below 20. It also confirmed common sense and popular opinion. So it is no surprise that the policy of small class sizes was adopted on a large scale in California given that funds were available.

But the hoped-for results did not occur. Exhaustive evaluations, ending with a third report in 2002 (Bohrnstedt and Stecher 2002) as rigorous as the Tennessee evaluation, could find no conclusive link in California between class-size reduction and student achievement. In particular, there was no greater effect among disadvantaged children.

I.A.1.3 What Went Wrong?

Why did these programs fail? This book will provide a general framework for understanding what went wrong in these two cases and what could go wrong in yours. This framework will provide you with the kinds of questions you need to answer to make better predictions about whether a proposed program will work for you if you implement it, and if you implement it how and when you would actually do so.

I.A.2 THE QUESTION, THE AUDIENCE, AND THE APPROACH

This book is concerned with one central question that should always be on the table in policy deliberation: Will it work here? That is, will the policy that you are considering make a positive difference in the desired outcome if you implement it, bearing in mind how, where, and when you would do so? In the language of the standard literature, this is a call for a prediction of *effectiveness*.

The book is designed for those who want to ensure that answers to this question are well warranted, or at least as well warranted as practical constraints allow, not just a matter of whim, or guess, habit, or political leaning; for those who want good arguments and good evidence to support the hopeful conclusion that the policy will work here if you undertake it. But we do not assume you are a scientist, or a statistician, or a methodologist. To the contrary, we aim to provide help for those who are not expert in these kinds of areas but who have to make policy decisions where getting it right about what will happen matters: classroom teachers thinking about homework, city councils deciding whether to build a leisure center, or government ministers contemplating drug policies.

Our book should help you make at least a rough estimate of how confident you are entitled to be that a proposed policy will achieve the targeted outcome should you implement it. We say "rough" estimate. We have in mind judgments like those suggested in the first reports of the International Panel on Climate Change (IPCC): "we are certain of . . .," "we calculate with confidence that . . .," "our judgement is that . . ." (Risbey and Kandlikar 2007: 20). Or, if you feel you can make finer gradations than that, like its 2006 categories: "Very high confidence," "High confidence," "Medium confidence," "Low confidence," "Very low confidence" (IPCC 2006: 3). We do not expect that you will generally be in a position to come up with numerical probabilities. But we do think you can often get into a position where you have a reasonable qualitative idea of how confident you should be.

The estimates, we shall argue, should be based on how sure you can be about the overall argument that supports the prediction that the policy will work here, as you would implement it. Are all the premises well warranted? Does the conclusion really follow from them—maybe you need to add some more premises to get the conclusion to follow. Then, how much warrant is there for these additional premises? Arguments, we stress, are like chains. They are only as strong as their weakest premise.

We shall start at the usual starting point for evidence-based policy: good studies that show that the policy worked somewhere. In part, because that is what you are enjoined to do if you are to engage in evidence-based policy but also because much effort has been put into gathering, evaluating, and cataloging these studies to make the fruits of current best science available to you. You don't have to be an expert. You don't have to dig the science out of the journals nor decide which results can be trusted and which are dicier. That has been done for you, by the US What Works Clearing House, for educational policy; the Jamil Poverty Action Lab (J-PAL) website in development economics; the Campbell Collaboration for education, crime and justice, and social welfare; and many others.[2]

We want to go well beyond that. Because "it worked somewhere" is just a starting point. It is a long road from "it works somewhere" to the conclusion you need—"it will work here," and it is not an easy one to traverse. In a sense that is well known. But what is known in principle often gets little attention in practice and there is surprisingly little guidance about how to proceed once you have launched out from the starting point. Take the US Department of Education website as an example. It says that you should look for strong evidence for your policy.[3] It then tells you that strong evidence equals two or more high quality RCTs. And you can find policies that have this kind of support in the What Works Clearing House. That's the starting point. So, what more do you need in order to have reasonable warrant for the prediction that the policy will work for you? The website tells you only that these RCTs should be carried out in "school settings similar to yours" (USDE 2003: 10), and that trials on white suburban populations do not constitute strong evidence for large inner-city schools serving primarily minority students. What's the general lesson here? Is there one?

We think there is. There are two further kinds of facts you will have to nail down, or nail down as best you can, to build a road from "it works somewhere" to "it will work here." These are, we shall show, facts about the causal role the policy plays and facts about the support factors that must be in place if the policy is to work. Without warrant for these, you don't have warrant for your prediction. That's what this book is about: getting all the way to "it will work here." We shall explain to you what we mean by causal roles and support factors, we will tell you why you should believe us when we say these are what you need to learn about, and we will provide advice for how to go about unearthing the facts that will provide decent warrant that your policy will work, here, in your situation, as you would implement it.

I.A.3 A STARTING POINT—BUT ONLY A STARTING POINT: THIS WORKED THERE

Before turning to what went wrong in California or in Bangladesh a prior question needs to be asked: Why should these programs have been expected to work in the first place? In both cases a good part of the answer is because they were well attested to have worked somewhere. Class-size reduction had produced good educational outcomes in 1985 in Tennessee—a fact attested to by a well-conducted RCT there. The Integrated Nutrition Program in Bangladesh was motivated in part by the success in Tamil Nadu, attested to by the World Bank Independent Evaluation Group report.

The policy worked there. That can be a natural starting point for thinking about whether the program will work for you. As Curtis Meinert, prominent clinical trials methodologist, says, "There is no point in worrying about whether a treatment works the same or differently in men and women until it has been shown to work on someone" (1995: 795).

A great deal of this book is devoted to the significance of "it worked there" if you are trying to bet whether "it will work here"—in our and the literature's language, the connection between evidence for *efficacy* and evidence for *effectiveness*. And that is why we start with two cases where the use of "it worked there" turned out to be problematic. And thinking of our readers, if you are following the dominant advice in evidence-based policy guidelines, you will have to start at this point, since these almost universally urge that you restrict yourself to programs that are established "to work." Which turns out to mean "it worked there": that is, in some particular setting, in some particular population, at some particular time. It also turns out to mean something narrower. The evidence that you have to have that "it works" cannot be just any old evidence. It should be evidence arrived at by using approved methods, and above all by using RCTs.

For readers well versed in the literature, the most salient feature of evidence-based policy is that predictions that a policy will work here, for you, should be based on the familiar evidence-ranking schemes and rigorous models for research synthesis, such as those of the Scottish Intercollegiate Guidelines Network or the Oxford Centre for Evidence-Based Medicine.[4] These look at study designs that support claims that a policy worked somewhere—there, in the study situation. The ranking schemes tell you what kinds of study designs are likely to make such claims *trustworthy*—you can rely on them to be most probably true. And they privilege RCTs as the best, the gold standard.

In PART IV we set out what we think is right and wrong with the rankings. And in I.B.5.3 we point out other very good sources of evidence for the same kinds of causal claims that the rankings deal with that do not appear in the standard lists at all. Ignoring them is throwing good, hard-won scientific knowledge into the bin. But our primary worries are more fundamental. No matter how much gold standard evidence you have for "it worked there," you cannot pave the road from there to here with gold bricks. PART II explains the materials you need: facts about causal roles here and there and facts about what support factors you have to have in place here.

The chapters of PART II are not about the familiar, practical problems that arise in the field when you are told that you have to use RCTs or similar—that there are none, or no good ones, and there couldn't be for moral or other reasons. Where that is so, a good reply to those who accuse RCT advocates of impracticality is that, if you don't have good evidence that the policy will work, perhaps you should not implement it. To do something when you do not know what will happen can be culpable, and it can have negative effects that you did not intend. Nor do we just commonsensically complain that by limiting yourself to RCTs you waste a lot of the evidence that as a matter of fact good practitioners rely on in the field. The purist can ask, in reply, whether we think that interventions should be based on bad evidence, on just any old evidence that people fall back on when they can't get the real thing?

We do not advocate bad evidence but rather good evidence that answers different questions. To support the prediction that the policy will work here where you are, you need to establish different kinds of facts. This book aims to tell you what these are and to provide advice about how to hunt them. Even where many good RCTs are available, and therefore the gold-standard evidence required by the conventional advice guides can be used, and therefore none of the practical concerns mentioned above apply, the RCT gives you only one of these kinds of facts: a richer version of "it worked there," this caused that there. This is of no value in helping discover the truth of all the other facts that you need in order to travel successfully to "it will work here."

We shall describe two kinds of searches you should make to collect the facts that are relevant to the transition from "this policy worked there" to "our proposed policy will work here": what we call "horizontal search" and "vertical search." But before describing these two kinds of searches, and giving case studies, we give a theoretical account of our approach. This is because we want to show that our approach is principled, not just a list of helpful tips. The ideas of horizontal and vertical search come from theory. Among other things, this shows that the solidity of your finishing point—a prediction that this program will probably work for you—depends on the solidity of all the essential ingredients. It does not depend just on the solidity of the point from which you start, that this worked somewhere.

An RCT gives you that important true fact, that this worked somewhere, and as we say, that may be a good starting point, not just because that is where the ranking schemes and the guidelines based on them have told you to start (and end). It can be very helpful to know that a program you are considering has very solid evidence to show that it worked somewhere. But that won't make for a secure conclusion if the evidence is weak in support of the right kinds of answers to the other questions you need to ask. A chain of argument is only as strong as its weakest link.

I.A.4 BRIEF PREVIEW

First, therefore, we have a theoretical discussion, in I.B, that indicates how predicting policy outcomes is really betting that the policy can play the right causal role in your situation and that your situation will have the right support factors to allow it to do so.

You may find this theoretical discussion a bit too dry and formal. That is intended. We want to state matters carefully and rigorously so you can be assured our recommendations are well grounded, and well grounded in a good general account of evidence, which is then specialized to the particular case of evidence for effectiveness. You can, if you wish, skip the body of the theory chapter and move directly to the bottom line, which we lay out more simply and less formally in I.B.7. Even that does not need to be digested to follow much of the rest of what we have to offer, since we have attempted to make the following chapters intelligible independent of the material in II.B that underwrites them.

I.B, including I.B.7, is theoretical. It provides an abstract, high-level framework to justify the conclusion that we should look for causal roles and support factors. In II.A and II.B, we explain what these are and why they matter, and describe two kinds of searches to find these two different kinds of facts that will help you predict more reliably whether your policy will work for you—horizontal search and vertical search. The ideas in II are explained informally and illustrated with practical examples so that they can be read and understood independent of their grounding in I.B. We introduce in II the two metaphors of causal cakes and of climbing up and down the ladder of abstraction, to illuminate how in practice you can think about what causal role your policy might play, and what support factors it will need in your specific context.

Next, in III, we set out four strategies to help with that thinking—pre-mortem (III.B.1); thinking step-by-step and thinking backwards (III.B.2); it works by means of what (III.B.3); and quick exit trees (III.B.4).

The theory in I.B aims to be rigorous and comprehensive. The metaphors and strategies in II and III are not. They are meant to help the practitioner to make the theory operational, to show how to think about what you need to know, or to bet on, when you are making particular effectiveness judgments. They are no more than heuristics, or tricks, or tips for making sense of what you have to decide. Not all will work in every circumstance, or for everybody. Other people will suggest other metaphors and strategies. Our suggestions do not therefore—and this is a major theme—provide a list of what you have to do if you are to think about effectiveness. We do not believe that such a list is possible.

PARTS II and III are the heart of the book. Even if you had read nothing of I.B, not even I.B.7, and you are not concerned with the wider comparisons and conclusions that we set out in IV and V, these chapters on their own will tell you how you should set about identifying the questions you need to answer in order to predict effectiveness reliably.

In IV we go back to where we start in I. In I, we acknowledge that the usual starting point for evidence-based policy is "good studies that show that the policy worked somewhere." What is meant by "good studies" is set out in a variety of evidence-ranking schemes, for example, those used by the US Department of Education's What Works Clearing House, in which RCTs appear as the gold standard. The claim is that, if you are looking for effectiveness, you can bet on a policy that is ranked highly by such schemes. In IV we look at how well, or as it turns out badly, RCTs and the guides and schemes and warehouses that privilege them can perform if you need help with our two questions: Will the policy play a causal role here? And, what support factors will it need in order to do so? This analysis reinforces the importance of the key distinction that we make between trustworthiness and relevance. What RCTs show brilliantly is that the policy did indeed work on average there, in that population, and therefore that it must have played a causal role there and had the support factors it needed. The RCT design makes these conclusions highly trustworthy. But RCTs cannot help with, and the ranking schemes do not concentrate on, the relevance of that success there for answering the two questions we say must be answered if you are looking for success here.

PART V considers the mandatory prescription of RCT-based policies as an example of a decentralization rule. In a system that needs to leave the execution of policy to others, it is tempting to impose rules to restrict the discretion of operatives on the ground. That reduces the opportunity to adopt bad policies. For this, it has to be possible to find a rule—for example, use only RCT-approved policies—that does indeed produce a good result in all, or most, or enough cases. We do not think that rule is a good rule, because we think that to decide about effectiveness requires an open-ended process of thinking that is inevitably contextual and cannot be reduced to rules. Mandating RCT-based policies selects in favor of operatives who are good at conforming with rules and against those who are good at thinking. But being good at thinking, for example, by using our metaphors and strategies, is what you need to produce reliable effectiveness predictions.

PART V.B looks at the wider implications for policy making, and in particular evidence-based policy, of our conclusions. In many cases it may be hard to answer the questions we think should be answered. It is possible that you just cannot understand well enough the causal roles that different factors play in (say) problem drug use, let alone what support factors are needed, let alone whether, as a matter of fact, those factors are likely to be present. So, at the very least, our way of thinking should lead to greater modesty among policy makers and, in particular, among politicians. If you don't know, the temptation to proceed anyway should be treated with suspicion. More positively, your policies should be flexible, not only to local circumstances, but to experience. But this caution should not be seen as conservative with respect to social policy. As compared with RCT-based rules, our approach may be liberating. For that orthodoxy, absence of a good RCT should be paralyzing. And in social policy there are, and can be, very few RCTs. But for us, absence of an RCT is not paramount, because for us, an RCT is just one way of seeing that it has worked somewhere, and that is a long way from saying that it will work here.

I.A.5 WHAT ISN'T HERE

Our effort is in the nature of a sketch. We hope that our success or failure will be judged accordingly, not by errors or shortcomings of detail in fact or reasoning—which will be many in a work that ranges from the formal qualities of RCTs to decentralization. We hope it will instead be judged by the extent to which we have focused attention on what it really means to use evidence for policy. Our book makes no pretense to comprehensiveness. It is organized around and gets its unity from one central theme: whether a policy will really work for you—what is called *effectiveness*.

In doing this, we say a lot about RCTs, because they figure so prominently in contemporary discussions of evidence and how to formulate policy based on good evidence. But we say nothing about the wide range of practical and theoretical problems associated with carrying out good RCTs. Some of these are admirably set out in the US Department of Education's guide to identifying rigorous evidence (USDE 2003). We proceed as though the quality control of the production of RCTs is of a very high standard. This is because our concern is with what you can do with an RCT once it has been produced—with what sort of evidence RCTs provide, and how relevant that is to making policy.

Nor do we discuss all those other also important questions you face in settling on policy. Our book does not deal with the money—it would be too expensive; with ideology/values/prejudices—you can't just double the number of prison places; popular opinion—eliminating free milk will cause an outcry; and a wide range of such factors that a full account of decision making would cover.

Nor do we help you choose goals or define them, which will involve a delicate balance between specifying the goals precisely enough to ensure you know what you are talking about and can monitor it, and ensuring that you do not settle on an only very partially reliable symptom of your real goal: you want your educational policy to contribute to students being better able to function as competent, contributing citizens. Should you settle, in the United Kingdom, on a measurable target of five C's at GCSE level? In the United States, on an 85% high school graduation rate?

The schema in figure I.1, from Davies 2005, provides a daunting picture of everything that generally needs to go into determining a policy decision.

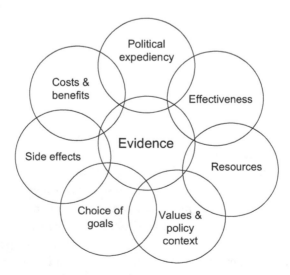

Figure I.1: Factors influencing policy making

Every circle needs evidence to support the claims that are made there, for example, about political expediency. But we are concerned only with what counts as good evidence for the top right circle, called *Effectiveness*—"it will work here." Although we deal with only this one corner of the decision problem, it is an important one—and a difficult one to get right. Our advice should make it a little easier.

CHAPTER I.B

⌇

The Theory That Backs Up What We Say

I.B.1 WHY DO WE WANT THEORY?

We began I.A with the examples of Bangladesh and California to show how carefully and intelligently chosen policies can fail, even though they are based on excellent evidence that the same policy has worked well elsewhere. The journey from "it worked there" to "it will work here" is not easy. In this chapter we want to set out the theory that lies behind our practical recommendations.

We do so because we want to show that our ideas about deciding policy are principled. Our approach is not just bluff and practical—the plain man's way of cutting through the complexity of statistical evidence, probability theory, and so on to hard, coal-face facts that will lead to realistic predictions. Our advice is rooted in a theory, a theory of *evidence for use*. This is a theory designed specifically for the user's problem of understanding what kinds of knowledge are good for reliable predictions about whether policies will work for you as you would implement them.

For evidence-based policy you need evidence that is both trustworthy and that speaks clearly for or against the policy. There are many sources available to help with the first of these: "When is an evidence claim trustworthy?" Various evidence-ranking schemes tell you how to sort evidence claims that can be trusted, claims that are very well-established, from ones that are more doubtful. Most of these schemes focus on one special kind of claim, that the policy works somewhere. They tell you what kind of study can nail that down—generally with RCTs and meta-analyses of RCTs as their gold standard for this—and what kind of studies lend some, but far less, credibility to a claim that the policy worked somewhere. And various policy clearinghouses—policy warehouses—will vet policies for you, to ensure that they are well evidenced to work somewhere.

We will not duplicate these efforts here. We are engaged in a different enterprise, one that helps carry you beyond the knowledge that the policy has indeed worked somewhere. Which facts speak for or against the policy working for you—meaning, do or don't lend credibility to it—and under what conditions?

We build our recommendations from a theory of relevance. Relevance matters because knowing the facts is not enough when it comes to assembling evidence. You need to know facts that bear on the truth of the policy prediction. Which facts speak for or against it? Suppose you had an encyclopedia with all the facts about the world in it, forgetting what that could possibly mean, including the facts that you get from RCTs. Which ones should you take note of? The encyclopedia would tell you what is true. It would not tell you what is relevant. Getting the right answers about relevance is important, and ensuring that these answers are well grounded and defensible is essential if policy is to be evidence-based. That is why we need a theory of relevance.

I.B.2 TWO ASSUMPTIONS

Our treatment of relevance for effectiveness predictions is based on two assumptions. One relates to evidence in general; the other is special to the use of evidence that "it works somewhere" to support predictions that "it will work here." It will take some explaining before we can tell you what they are.

I.B.2.1 Assumption 1

I.B.2.1.a What Makes for Warrant?

To warrant a claim is to justify taking it to be true. So, how do you warrant the prediction that your proposed policy will work here, where you are? Warranting a claim, any claim, means marshaling reasons for it so that it is transparent why you have the right to be confident that the claim is true. It follows that *warrant requires a good argument*. An argument here is a set of propositions, called its *premises*, and a proposition, called its *conclusion*, not, as typically in ordinary language, just a reason ("My argument for buying this wine is that it is cheap"). The reasons you marshal must themselves be trustworthy and together they should compel the conclusion, or at least make it likely. That's what we mean by a *good argument*. A good argument is both sound and valid. *Sound* means that the premises are trustworthy; *valid*, that the conclusion is genuinely implied by the premises. Good arguments provide strong warrant for their conclusions; the weaker the argument, the weaker the warrant.

If the conclusion of an argument is to be well warranted, each of its premises must be well warranted as well. Some premises may be self-evident, or already well established, or attested to by a reliable expert, or just easy to tell by looking. For instance, from our discussion of CCTV cameras and car crime in III.B.3.1, it does not take a major study to support the claim that your parking lot is surrounded by an 8-foot high wall nor an intimate knowledge of physiology and criminal sociology to know that most car thieves cannot readily leap 8-foot walls. To know whether CCTV footage is admissible in court, ask a lawyer. And if it happens that a premise in your argument is that a policy has worked somewhere, for warrant you can take the word of a good policy warehouse, like What Works or the Campbell Collaboration. Often, however, the premises in your main argument—call these *major premises*—will themselves need serious support. So you will need subarguments, each with its own premises, to support the major premises. Maybe you will even need subarguments to the subarguments. Each argument and each subargument must be a good one—valid and sound—or the whole structure is threatened.

Sometimes a variety of different arguments can be offered in support of the same conclusion. This is typical when premises are insecure. You hope that at least one of your arguments can stand firm. What's doing the justificatory work in this case is yet another argument with yet further premises. It looks like this: "The premises of Argument 1, if true, make the conclusion probable; the premises of Argument 2, if true, make the conclusion probable; . . . the premises of Argument N, if true, make the conclusion probable. Probably the premises of at least one of Arguments 1, 2, . . ., N are true. Therefore the conclusion is probably true." This is fine, so long as you are clear about just what the overall argument is and about how secure its premises are. Otherwise there is danger that you will over—or under—bid your cards.

To get clear on just what your argument is, one device you can employ is to build an argument pyramid, as in figure I.2. The conclusion is at the top. The major premises are the next layer down. Below each major premise are the premises in the subargument that supports it. And below each of those, the premises of the sub-subargument that supports it. Put blank boxes where you can see you need more premises to make a valid argument

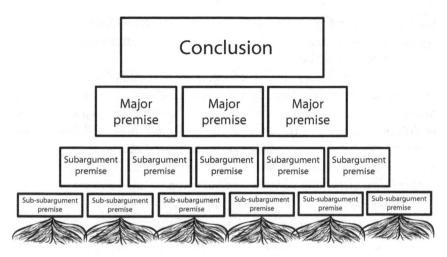

Figure I.2: What argument pyramids look like

but don't know just what they are. For instance, Inspector French's argument that Carey killed Ackerly, which we discuss in I.B.2.1.b, might require a motive for the killing. If French suspects there is a good motive, but doesn't have a good hypothesis about what it is yet, he would leave the space for that premise blank. Stop when you run out of arguments or don't need them anymore. From any premises that don't need further serious support—like those that are self-evident or that you just see by looking or are already well established or attested to by a reliable expert—draw roots into the ground. This is to show that they can stand on their own.

There are two big advantages to taking seriously the connection between argument and warrant and to sketching argument pyramids like this. First, it helps you put order into your reasons. Second, it helps you assess the degree of confidence you should have in your conclusion. Ideally every box is filled in and every box stands on others and those on others until eventually all are rooted in the ground. Then you can have a high degree of confidence in your conclusion. If lots of boxes are hanging in the air and there are lots of blank boxes as well, your degree of confidence should be low.

Often you will find the pyramid is shaky, but it doesn't seem too implausible to think that the rest, with world enough and time, could be filled in and supplied with thick roots at the bottom. That justifies some confidence, but not a high degree. If you find yourself in this situation—as we suspect you very often will—you should not despair. This is the typical human condition; relative certainty is hard to come by. You can then decide whether the policy is worth pursuing given that it may well be effective, but then again, it may well not. And at least you will have a better estimate of how confident you should be.

There is one caution in the use of argument pyramids. The visual representation can be misleading. Suppose you have an argument with three major premises. If you take away the one that you have pictured in the middle, it can look as if the conclusion is still well supported. But, to the contrary. Where there are blank boxes there are holes in the argument, and an argument with holes provides no support at all. You only get some support if you hypothesize that these holes can be filled in. And your support for the conclusion can be no stronger than your justification for this hypothesis.

I.B.2.1.b Evidence and Argument

We now turn to evidence. The evidence for a claim is supposed to help provide warrant for it; it is supposed to help justify your confidence that the claim is true. That means that evidence must figure in a good argument. The evidence claim must appear as a major premise—or a subpremise, or a sub-subpremise—in an argument alongside other premises that together make the conclusion probable. That's what secures relevance. It is the overall argument that turns one of those millions of trustworthy claims one can make about the world into a piece of evidence for the conclusion. This means that whether a particular claim is evidence for a conclusion depends on some specific argument for the conclusion in which that claim figures and on how good that argument is.

Evidential relevance then is a three-place relation. It involves an evidence claim, a hypothesis (or conclusion), and an argument: claim *e* is evidence for hypothesis *h relative to some good argument A*. Relative to the argument under consideration, some evidence claims will be what we call *directly relevant*; others only *indirectly relevant*. The claims expressed in the major premises of the argument are what we label *directly relevant* to the hypothesis. But we know that if the hypothesis is to be well-warranted, each of the major premises must itself be well-warranted, so each of these too must have a good argument to support it. Any of the claims offered as premises in one of these subarguments are, in our terminology, *indirectly relevant* to the original hypothesis. This carries on, generating evidence claims that are relevant to the original hypothesis, but more and more indirectly, and relative to a series of arguments connecting them to it.

This gives us a good, succinct account of evidential relevance, that is, an account of what turns a trustworthy claim into a piece of evidence. It is the first assumption of our theory:

Assumption 1

A well-established empirical claim e is evidence for h if and only if e can be rendered as a premise in an argument, A, and A is a good argument for h; or, e is a premise in A′, where A′ is a good argument for a premise in a good argument, A, for h; and so forth.

As we urged in the last section, it is important to be clear just what the arguments are for your conclusion and how well supported their premises are in order to assess how confident you can be that the conclusion is correct. An argument pyramid with gaps where you don't know just what form one of the essential premises takes provides shaky support for your conclusion. It's far worse when you have good reason to think one of the essential premises is false. We stress the importance of arguments because arguments, like chains, are only as strong as their weakest link. A valid argument with nine premises known to be true and one known to be false does not make its conclusion 90% probable. It provides no warrant at all. So a body of evidence that nails down nine of the premises is not enough for high warrant. Indeed, if the tenth premise is known to be false, the argument is no good at all and the proffered "evidence" is irrelevant to the truth of the conclusion. This is important to keep in mind for evidence-based policy, where some of the premises may be very well established but often others may be fairly dicey. In this case you must be careful not to overestimate the warrant you have for your policy predictions.

Mystery stories can provide good examples of the importance of each premise to the stability of the overall structure. Consider Freeman Wills Croft's Inspector French, who is always at pains to lay out clearly the arguments that support his conclusions. In *Death On the Way*, Inspector French has become convinced, on the basis of a body of seemingly good evidence, that Carey murdered Ackerly. We reconstruct his warrant for this in the form we advocate—that of an argument with explicit premises and explicit subpremises.

Premise 1 in French's argument concerns motive. Ackerly, French argued, had cottoned on to a major fraud that Carey was involved in. This was backed by compelling evidence for three claims: fraud had been committed; Ackerly had raised suspicions about it; and Carey was responsible for the fraud. This last was supported by evidence that Carey was in a position to perpetrate the fraud, that he had income otherwise unaccounted for, and, very importantly, that he had committed suicide when it looked as if the fraud might be revealed despite Ackerly's death.

There was equally good evidence for Premise 2 concerning opportunity. Carey *could* have committed the murder. We won't tell the whole story here: the check marks in figure I.3 mean that French did indeed have good reasons to back his claim about Carey's opportunity. But opportunity and motive by themselves do not support a conclusion of guilt. French, though, had a third premise. Premise 3 laid out the method. This was a step-by-step narrative, of the kind we discuss in III.B.2, of how Carey was supposed to have carried out the murder. This narrative was supported by good evidence that Carey was at some of the right places at the right times, and French had established, by timing distances and estimating speeds, that Carey could have been at the other places in the chain just when needed. We graph French's reasoning in the argument pyramid picture in figure I.3. French had a way to fill in all the boxes all the way down, but we won't do so since the details for them do not matter to the story.

Together French's three major premises made a compelling argument for Carey's guilt—seemingly both sound and valid. Then it was revealed that Carey had not committed suicide but rather was murdered. French immediately reported this to his superior. Here is a record of their conversation, beginning with a question from French's superior (Crofts 2001: 202):

> "This is going to mean an upset to your theory, Inspector?"
>
> French nodded. "Complete. I've got to start from the beginning again."
>
> "Is it as bad as that?"
>
> "... I think so. .... This murder of Carey makes it unlikely that he killed Ackerly, and if he didn't kill Ackerly, the whole of my theory goes west."

So, the whole theory falls. There is no longer compelling reason to think that Carey murdered Ackerly.

But what about all that evidence that French had so painstakingly gathered? It was no longer evidence that Carey was the killer. The suicide was

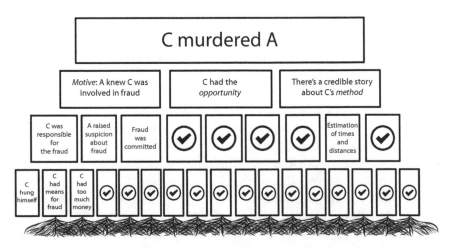

Figure I.3: The argument pyramid supporting French's accusation of Carey

an essential prop for the assumption that Carey was responsible for the fraud. Without the suicide, the other evidence for this was just far too weak to justify that assumption. But without it, Premise 1 fails—motive is not established. And without motive, opportunity and the existence of a possible method for carrying out the murder provide weak warrant, if any at all, that Carey was the murderer. It is still possible that he was guilty. But French no longer has evidence to support that. Evidence is a three-place relation. The measurements of distances and times are evidence of Carey's guilt, yes; but only relative to French's entire argument. When one of the necessary premises in that argument fails, those measurements are no longer evidence at all.[1] As French says, his whole theory collapses—as in figure I.4.

Before turning to our second assumption, some remarks on terminology are in order. Sometimes "evidence" is used in a broader sense than ours. For instance, historian of physics Peter Galison argues that mathematics is the new laboratory of physics. In some branches of physics, like string theory, often the best evidence that a theory is on the right track is not whether it predicts new experimental results but rather whether its equations satisfy certain abstract mathematical constraints, often having to do with symmetries (Galison 2004). When we use the term "evidence" we mean something narrower; we mean *empirical evidence*. Whether the facts are local, like "there is an 8-foot wall around our parking lot," or very general, like the law of gravitational attraction, for us evidence claims report facts about the world.

Others use the term "evidence" more narrowly than we do. Evidence claims are restricted to reports of the results of individual scientific studies. We reject this usage because our topic is evidence for predicting effectiveness, and the context is evidence-based policy. There is a general assumption about evidence-based policy that if you have a great deal of trustworthy

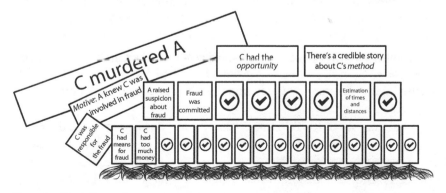

Figure I.4: The collapse of an accusation

evidence, you are in a good position to predict whether the policy will work here. But if evidence is restricted to just results of individual scientific studies, this assumption is badly mistaken. You need a lot more facts than specific results of specific scientific studies to argue that a policy will work here. You need, as we shall show, facts about causal roles and about support factors—that's what our book is about. Without these facts, and without good warrant for them, your conclusion is not justified. If evidence-based policy is to do its job then, it is best to construe evidence widely enough to cover all the facts without which you will not have a good argument.

I.B.2.2 Assumption 2

We begin with the observation that evidential relevance depends on the type of hypothesis. Different types of hypotheses require different types of evidence. The hypotheses that we are concerned with in this book—policy effectiveness predictions—are causal claims: the proposed policy will *cause* an improvement in the targeted outcome if you implement it. That's part of why you are willing to adopt the policy—because you expect it to make a difference.

The most straightforward argument to support the truth of a prediction is one that lays out the facts that would make that prediction come true. We are going to focus on this kind of argument because it is special: its premises must be true or the prediction won't come true; if any of the premises fail, so too will the conclusion. When the conclusion is a prediction about what effects a policy would have in a given situation, these are the facts about the situation that ensure that the policy would produce the specified effect there. What are these?

We suppose that causes do not produce their effects by accident, at least not if you are to be able to make reliable predictions about what will happen if you intervene. Rather, if a cause produces an effect, it does so because there is a reliable, systematic connection between the two, a connection that is described in a *causal principle*. Our advice is grounded in basic assumptions about these causal principles and how they operate, which we describe below. Facts about these principles will play an essential role in the argument that justifies the prediction that the policy will work here, where you are.

What then about RCTs? How do they figure in our story about the need for a good argument and about the importance of citing facts about causal principles among the premises in arguments for policy effectiveness? After all, RCTs, and related studies that provide strong warrant that the policy worked somewhere, are the conventional focal point of evidence-based policy. If your argument for policy effectiveness does not include evidence of this kind, you will probably be judged not to be doing evidence-based policy. And we agree that starting here can be a good idea, especially now that so many warehouses for vetting and storing this kind of evidence are available. So how do you get RCTs to figure in a good argument for effectiveness?

RCTs show that a policy works somewhere. That's supposed to be one premise. What other premises are needed alongside this to produce a good argument that the policy will work here? This is our second assumption:

Assumption 2

To get a good argument from "it works somewhere" to "it will work here" facts about causal principles here and there are needed.

Otherwise, there is no good way to make the study results relevant to predictions about what will happen were the policy to be implemented in the target setting. Our approach is based on identifying just what facts about causal principles are needed to fill in the missing premises. Our advice throughout is principled in that it is based on an account of causation that is intellectually robust and that translates into practical suggestions for ways to recognize the facts that are relevant to policy prediction.

I.B.3 CAUSAL PRINCIPLES

I.B.3.1 What Is a Causal Principle?

We take from recent philosophical work on causality a few basic assumptions about the kinds of causal principles that typically support reliable policy prediction.

1. Causal principles do not record mere statistical associations; "correlation is not causation." That's because causes make their effects happen; they contribute to their production; they are responsible for them. That's the point of adopting a policy. The policy should make a difference. And that should not just be a matter of chance.

2. There may be some causal principles that hold everywhere; perhaps the law of gravitational attraction, that two masses attract each other with a force GMm/r^2, is an example. But this is not typical in the sciences and especially not in the medical and social sciences. In these areas, principles can vary from one situation to another; they can be more or less general; and more or less deep. In PART II we shall be reminded how the fact that causal principles can differ from locale to locale means that you cannot read off that a

policy will work here from even very solid evidence that it worked somewhere else, or even in a number of somewhere elses.

3. Causal principles are not all on a par. Some may be more fundamental than others. The less fundamental hold *on account of* the more fundamental; with the right additional assumptions about local structure, they can be *derived from* the more fundamental ones. Generally the more fundamental hold more widely. Planets circulate around the sun in elliptical orbits that are described by Kepler's laws. But the orbits are also described by Newton's more fundamental laws and, with background assumptions about the starting velocities and masses and their arrangement, Kepler's laws can be derived from Newton's. Kepler's elliptical orbits are the working out of Newton's laws when planets interact with the sun; they are what Newton's laws amount to given the structure and features of the planetary system. This classic case is from physics. But the same kind of layering of principles occurs in the biological and social realm. In II.B, we shall see how this fact can sometimes provide a powerful tool for constructing new, different programs from ones that worked elsewhere or for avoiding failures, as in the Bangladesh Integrated Nutrition Project.

4. The causal principles employed throughout the biological, medical, and social sciences are ceteris paribus principles. They hold only with "other things being equal," or, to put it more accurately, with other things being "normal," or "within appropriate bounds." This is familiar. Reducing class sizes will not help reading scores if a hurricane wipes out the schools.

5. Causal principles can be deterministic, as in classical physics, where the causes fix exactly what effects must occur. They may be merely probabilistic, as in dicing or quantum mechanics, where a given effect occurs with some fixed probability. Or, as in our more general experience, they may be even less regimented than that. The effects occur sometimes, or more often than not, or most of the time. They may also be quantitative, expressed in equations; they can alternatively be qualitative, relating features that do not have exact quantitative measures.

6. As we explain with simple examples in II.A, generally for the kinds of effects aimed for in policy planning:
   a. contributions to the effect can come from different sources and via different pathways;
   b. the overall effect depends in some systematic way on the contributions from these separate sources—in the simplest case the contributions simply add up; and
   c. in general social policies are not enough by themselves to ensure a contribution to the targeted effect; the policy described needs the right *support team* before it can be expected to produce a contribution.

Philosophers have a technical term to summarize (6), which we shall explain in detail in II.A. They say, "Causes are INUS conditions for their effects."[2] An INUS condition is an Insufficient but Necessary part of an Unnecessary but Sufficient condition for producing a contribution to the effect. We introduce this philosopher's edict because it underlines two important facts to keep in mind in evaluating whether a policy will work here.

First, the program or policy under consideration will seldom be sufficient by itself, no matter how much effort has been taken to include in its description as much as possible of what is required. The policy will only be a *part* of a team of causes that work together. It takes the whole team to produce a contribution. Together, the factors in the team are Sufficient for a contribution. But the separate team members, though Necessary for that team to produce a contribution, are each by itself Insufficient for doing so.

The reminder that a policy under consideration is generally just part of a team and is insufficient by itself to produce a contribution focuses attention on the questions: Are the requisite team members—which we call *support factors*—at hand? If not, can they be introduced practicably? There may, of course, be more than one set of support factors that will round out a policy to form a complete team, in which case the questions is: Are there to hand all of the factors required in at least one team in which the policy figures?

Second, the team in which the policy figures will not generally be the only thing that could contribute to the outcome. The team with the policy in it is Unnecessary for a contribution since a number of other teams that may or may not contain the policy can also contribute. The actual value of the outcome in a situation will depend on all the teams that operate in that situation, and on the size and direction of the contribution from each. Some of these will contribute positively and some negatively.

To estimate the *value of the outcome* after the policy, you need to catalog all those factors that will be operating to produce the effect, which is a tall order. Plus you will need some formula for calculating how they combine, how they "add up."[3] You will need to do a little less if you want to predict by *how much matters will be different after the policy*, since for this you need to consider the effects only of teams containing factors that change, but you will need to consider both those that change as a result of your actions and those that change independently of what you do. To predict instead whether and how much things will change *as a result of the policy and its implementation*, you only need to know about the teams that include factors that you will be changing—both those that contain the policy itself and also any others that you may change during implementation. We discuss post-implementation effects further in I.B.4. For the more restricted prediction of just *what the policy itself does*, independent of any other changes introduced in implementing it, you need only look at teams with the policy in them.

Even for these final two more typical and somewhat easier exercises, though, it is not always safe to ignore teams that you won't be changing. For instance, if there are already present teams that produce very large contributions, your policy may make such a negligible difference that it is not worth pursuing. There is no point in feeding the prisoner a meal low in salt and fat in order to improve her health if she is to be executed the next morning.

7. There can be different rules for how contributions combine depending on what the subject matter is. The social sciences often assume simple addition. Even there, though, allowance is made for threshold and marginal effects: if the outcome reaches a certain size, additional contributions make no difference, or each new unit may make less difference than the one before. In mechanics, forces combine by vector addition. In econometrics, sometimes the contribution of each separate factor is represented in a different equation. When the factors all act together, the separate equations must all be satisfied at once. And in both physics and economics, it is often supposed that the net outcome will be some kind of equilibrium among the various contributions.

Even though many of the causal principles that ground policy predictions may be purely qualitative, as explained in (5), much of the standard literature supposes that principles can be expressed in equations. We shall focus on principles like this in order to exploit some of the ideas and derivations already available in this literature. For similar reasons we shall focus on equations in which contributions from different sources simply add, despite the more complicated rules for combination noted in (7). We shall also, as is standard, suppose the equations are deterministic, despite the cautions in (5). Without these simplifications, technical matters become more complicated. But the basic lessons we draw remain the same.

Given these simplifying assumptions, we can suppose that the causal principles for the production of an outcome *y* look like this:

$$CP : y(i)c = a_1 + a_2 y_0(i) + a_3 b(i)x(i) + a_4 z(i),[4]$$

where the *i*'s range over the individuals in the population to which the principle applies (these could be anything from individual students to classrooms or states), *y(i)* is the outcome, *x(i)* is the policy variable, *a*'s are constants across all individuals, $y_0(i)$ is a "base level" of y for i, $b(i)$ represents all the different factors in all the support teams that work with x to ensure a contribution for i, and $z(i)$ represents, in one fell swoop, all the other factors and their support teams that contribute additively with x but do not include x. a_2, a_3, and a_4 represent what might be called "boost factors"; they fix the size of the contribution from given values of the variables that follow. (These are like the constant of gravity, G, in the force of gravitational attraction between two masses: GMm/r^2.) We employ the symbol $c =$ to represent that the quantities on the two sides are equal and that the ones on the right side are causes of the one on the left.

I.B.3.2 An Illustration

To illustrate, here is a simplified version of one of the examples that we use in II.A, where we set out the causal cake metaphor as a more user friendly way of approaching the notion of INUS conditions. We emphasize later that premature or optimistic simplification is in general risky in thinking about social policy—much of the problem is that you can forget too readily how many and how various are the other factors that have to be present if your policy is to work. So the simplified version here must be seen as no more than an attempt to clarify the notion of an INUS condition, which is a long way from the complexities of a discussion of what actually has to be done when you are to make that notion operative in the field.

Consider the case of Tamil Nadu, where infant health ($i.h.$) was improved by educating mothers about nutrition. We shall take this result as given. How can that be expressed in terms of our equation CP? Like this:

$$\text{TN}: i.h.(i)\ c = a_1 + a_2 i.h._0(i) + a_3 b_m(i)\, e_m(i) + a_4 z(i),$$

where e_m is educating the mother, and we know what that means. But the other factors are unknowns.

Suppose, just so that you can see what is at stake, the effectiveness of e_m in Tamil Nadu has been very well established via a very good RCT. A positive effect in the RCT in Tamil Nadu tells you two things: that e_m is a member of some team of factors, b_m and e_m, that produced a positive contribution to infant health for some individuals under the causal principle that obtained in Tamil Nadu; and that the support factors for e_m required under that principle, represented by b_m (whatever they may be), were present in Tamil Nadu. In the terminology we shall employ, e_m *played a positive causal role* for some individuals in Tamil Nadu. This means no more than what the RCT tells you. It does not tell you what causal principle was operating there, nor anything about the other factors that affected the outcomes in the individuals in the study (represented by z), nor anything about the support factors represented in b_m, except that they were present, nor about the boost factor a_2.

You now go to Bangladesh and educate mothers in nutrition, betting on an equation like TN:

$$BD: i.h.(i) \; c = a_1' + a_2' \; i.h._0(i) + a_3' b_m(i)' e_m(i) + a_4' z.'$$

We write a_1' and so on rather than a_1 because here, too, you do not know what a_1' and so on stand for. But whatever they stand for, there is no reason to think that it is the same as in TN. Nor, more important, do you know whether b_m', which represents the support factors for e_m, is the same as b_m.

Post hoc evaluations indicate that the program had little effect on infant health in Bangladesh. There are then two possibilities:

1. That e_m does indeed form part of the applicable causal principle BD, but the support factors were not present.
2. That e_m does not even appear in the causal principle, so the question of the presence or absence of support factors, such as b_m and b_m', does not arise.

In cases like (1), we will use language like "*could* play a positive causal role." It actually *does* play a positive causal role only if the support factors are present as well. In cases like (2), there is no question of either an actual or a potential causal role.

In both cases, you have in practice to think about what may be the evidence for a particular policy being part of an applicable causal principle. You have also to think about what evidence there may be for this or that being a support factor; and what evidence there may be that those support factors are present in your situation. The nature of the evidence will in general be very different in each case. For example, science may tell you that this policy is part of a causal principle here, whereas the evidence required to know that a known support factor is present may be no more than the evidence before your eyes.

The distinction also matters when you think about what might have gone wrong in Bangladesh. If you spot that the mother was certainly educated and that could have contributed to *i.h.*, but there was not enough, or not the right kind, of food for her education to pay off, then you have case (1): e_m is in the causal principle, but you did not have b_m'. But if you see that the mother is not in charge of handing out the food, but the mother-in-law is, you have case (2), and e_m is not relevant, so the presence of $b_m{}'$ does not arise. You might in that case consider the following:

$$BD: i.h.(i) \ c = a_1{}' + a_2{}' \ i.h._0(i) + a_3{}'' b_{ml}(i)e_{ml}(i) + a_4{}'z'(i)$$

where e_{ml} is *educate the mother-in-law*. And a'' and so on instead of a' or a signals that you don't know what a'' stands for and certainly don't know that a and a' and a'' and so on are the same. And the same in the case of the support factors, b_{ml}, for educating mothers-in-law in Bangladesh. They may not be at all the same as for educating mothers in Tamil Nadu, or mothers-in-law in charge of households elsewhere.

If educating the mother-in-law works, you have two equations:

$$BD: \ i.h.(i) \ c = a_1{}' + a_2{}' \ i.h._0(i) + a_3{}'' b_{ml}(i)e_{ml}(i) + a_4{}'z'(i)$$

$$TN: \ i.h.(i) \ c = a_1 + a_2 i.h._0(i) + a_3 \ b_m(i)e_m(i) + a_4 z(i).$$

They represent two causal principles with nothing in common except their abstract form. If without doing any more testing you write e_{pw}, meaning *educate the person with the power*, for both e_m and e_{ml}, you get:

$$TN: \ i.h.(i) \ c = a_1 + a_2 i.h._0(i) + a_3{}''' b_{pw}(i)e_{pw}(i) + a_4 z(i)$$

$$BD: \ i.h.(l) \ c = a_1{}' + a_2{}' \ i.h._0(i) + a_3{}''''b'_{pw}(i)e_{pw}(i) + a_4{}'(i)z'(i).$$

These represent two causal principles with one thing (and only one thing) in common, the intervention e_{pw}. Even the support factors for educating the person in power might be different between Tamil Nadu and Bangladesh, hence b_{pw} and $b_{pw}{}'$ in the two principles.

As II.B shows, this transformation, which appears to amount to no more than inserting mother and mother-in-law each into her equation under another, common, description, is more than just a smart way of creating causal principles that have something in common. As the modest process of reflection described above shows, thinking like that can lead you to the mother-in-law. And in parts of Africa it may lead you to the elder sister.

I.B.4 WHAT MAKES EFFECTIVENESS PREDICTIONS TRUE?

Recall our second assumption: to get a good argument from "it works there" to "it will work here," facts about causal principles here and there are needed. Just which facts about causal principles are these? Start with the prediction that the policy will work here. The answer to our question depends on just what is meant by "will work here." What the facts are that will make an effectiveness prediction true depends on exactly what form the prediction takes, that is, on just what you want to predict about the outcome after policy implementation.

Below we present a catalog for a variety of familiar predictions that you might want to make. For the most part, in this book we focus on the last, minimal, prediction: "the policy will contribute positively here." As you see from the catalog, this is the weakest of the effectiveness predictions you might want to make, and the factors you need to know about for this conclusion are essential for all the others. For instance, to predict that the overall difference due just to the policy itself is positive, you will need to know about all the positive contributions it makes, and all the negative, and that the positive outweigh the negative. The lessons we propose about warrant for this minimal prediction are then all relevant when it comes to warrant for the stronger predictions. You will need at least the information we propose plus more if you want a stronger conclusion.

1. Almost always the most difficult thing to predict, even if you are prepared to admit a reasonable degree of error, is the actual value of the outcome, individual by individual. There are two kinds of facts that are responsible for what the actual value will be for an individual unit i:
   - The causal principle for the production of y that obtains after implementation.
   - The values for the given individual of all the quantities occurring in that principle.
2. Predicting the average outcome across the individuals in the population, though not so demanding, is still incredibly difficult. There are two kinds of facts that are responsible for the average outcome value:
   - The causal principle that obtains after implementation.
   - The averages across the population of all the terms occurring in that principle.
3. Often you would be pleased to predict with some confidence that the outcome average will be better if you adopt the policy than if you don't, rather than predicting the actual average that would occur. In many cases this can be easier. But it can sometimes be tricky. The tricky part comes if the causal principle governing the production of the effect changes in the course of policy implementation.

   The possibility of changes in the course of policy implementation is an important feature of how the world works, not at all an unusual occurrence. A good many of the causal principles that produce the outcomes of interest in policy deliberation are not basic laws of nature but are derivative. They express what more fundamental principles give rise to in particular structures. When you implement policy you can change these structures and thus change the very principles you were hoping to rely on to predict the outcomes of your interventions.

This is one of the fundamental reasons that the Chicago School in economics urged against government intervention. Robert Lucas, in what has become famous as "the Lucas critique" (1976), made just this claim. He produced models of interacting economic agents that—*if* the models are correct—show that the very fact that the government manipulates a cause, as opposed to the cause taking its "natural" value, will change the underlying structure so that it will no longer give rise to the principle used for policy prediction. His now classic example is of the Phillips curve, which relates inflation to unemployment—a relationship that Lucas argues breaks down when politicians attempt to reduce unemployment by manipulating inflation.

What Lucas claims happens with the Phillips curve can happen any-where. In our BINP and TINP examples, educating the mother or the mother-in-law may make them feed the children better. But they may also get the idea from other members of the group where they are educated that they might get a job and hand over giving out the food to the eldest child. You have then, perhaps unintentionally, changed the social struc-ture. Educating the mother or the mother-in-law may no longer work because the old causal principles no longer apply given the new social structure. Educating the mother or the mother-in-law will no longer play a causal role in contributing to children's nutrition because it is not in the new causal principle, although educating the eldest child may be.

In cases such as these where the causal principle changes under policy implementation, the average difference will be the difference between the average that would have been produced under the principle that would have obtained were the policy not implemented minus the out-come average under the new principle. So the facts responsible for the average difference are:

- The old principle.
- The new principle.
- The averages of all the terms that differ between the two supposing, for the old principle, that the policy is not implemented and, for the new, that it is.

4. If the causal principle does not change, the facts that determine the difference between outcome averages are:

- The averages that would obtain were the policy not implemented, for all the terms whose averages change.
- The averages that would obtain were the policy implemented, for all the terms whose averages change.

Notice that we mention "all the terms whose averages change." This is important because, as our discussion of the California class-size reduction program illustrates, often in implementing policy you change more causes than just the ones described in the policy, sometimes wittingly, but, if you are inattentive or unlucky, you can easily do so unwittingly. In principles of form CP, the difference in average outcomes with and without the policy will depend on the differences in the averages of the factors represented in $b(i)$ and $z(i)$.

5. You might be interested in what difference just the policy itself would contribute on average and supposing the causal principles stay the same, rather than what the average difference would be if the policy were implemented versus if it were not. That is, you may not be concerned about the difference in outcome average due to changes in any of the other causal factors that might change during implementation or due to changes in the causal principles themselves. This difference, when evaluated for a situation S, is often called the *efficacy* of the policy in S. Notice how slight, in terms of our taxonomy, is the significance of efficacy so defined.

   Sometimes you may be interested in the efficacy of the policy in S because you think of implementing the same policy again in S, keeping the causal principles there fixed, or of implementing it somewhere else where the same principles obtain as obtain in S, but this time implementing it in a different way, perhaps in a way that keeps all other causal factors fixed or improves their values. The efficacy of the policy measures just how much the policy itself contributes, averaged over all the individuals in the population under study. How interesting that is depends on how much you can rely on the fixity of the causal principles and factors. The factors that determine efficacy are:

   - The causal principle that holds, which by hypothesis is supposed to stay the same before and after implementation.
   - The average across the values of the support factors for the policy under that principle.

I.B.5 RCTs

We focus on relevance; the well-known ranking schemes focus on trustworthiness, and especially on the trustworthiness of claims that a policy or program worked somewhere, where RCTs and meta-analyses of RCTs are taken to be the best supporting evidence for such claims. Here we bring together these two projects and show how they relate. The central question for us is: Under what circumstances is an RCT evidentially relevant to an effectiveness prediction? We begin by explaining what an RCT is and why it is thought to be superior to other studies. Then we will investigate just what it is that an RCT can establish. But to be evidentially relevant, an RCT has not just to establish a fact, but offer what any other source of evidence must offer—support for a premise in an argument that leads to a conclusion. So in I.B.6 we will describe how to make RCT results relevant to your effectiveness prediction by showing how to bring them into your argument that the policy will work here, in your setting.

I.B.5.1 What Is an RCT?

An RCT is a study design based on John Stuart Mill's *method of difference* for making causal inferences (Mill [1843] 1850: bk. III, ch. 8). Mill's method-of-difference supposes, as we do here, that effects are produced in accord with causal principles. The causal principles for a given kind of situation or population, S, say what the causes of a given effect in S are, what each contributes, and how they combine. A method-of-difference study then aims to compare individual units that are the same with respect to all causal factors relevant to the given effect except the one in question, by which they differ. If individuals that are otherwise the same differ in values for the effect, then the factor by which they differ must be among the genuine causes of the effect under the principles governing S.

It is difficult to conduct a straightforward method-of-difference study, since it is so seldom known what all the factors for a given effect are, bar one. A familiar strategy for coping with this ignorance is to compare, not pairs of individuals, one-by-one, but rather two groups of individuals, one where the putative cause occurs, which is called *the treatment group,* and one where it does not, called *the control group*. Both groups are supposed to be subject to the same causal principle for the effect in question, and the distribution of causal factors other than the one in question between the two groups is (near enough) identical. For principles of form CP, that means that the distributions of y_0, b, and z are the same. Then if the two differ in the distribution of values for the effect, the putative cause must be a genuine cause for at least some members of the population.

It is naturally difficult to set up such a study since, in general, not all the causal factors relative to an outcome are known, which makes it hard to check that they are distributed equally in the two groups. Moreover differences between the treatment and control are easy to introduce in setting up the two groups (by, for instance, unconscious bias in selecting to which group to assign an individual) or in implementing the treatment (consider, e.g., the placebo effect). RCTs are supposed to help with just this problem.

An RCT is a Mill's method-of-difference group study in which individual units, all of which are supposed to be governed by the same causal principle, are randomly assigned to the treatment and control groups. There is also as much masking as possible—those delivering the treatment don't know which group an individual is in, nor those receiving it, those diagnosing whether or to what degree the effect occurs, those doing the statistical analysis, and so on. Finally the groups are supposed to be big enough to allow reliable inference from the observed frequencies to the true probabilities.

The random assignment plus masking are supposed to make it likely that the two groups have the same distribution of causal factors. It is controversial how confident these measures should make us that they do this.[5] This issue bears on the trustworthiness of causal claims backed by RCTs. As we noted, trustworthiness is the central topic of many other guides. But we aim to move beyond that; we concentrate on relevance. In order to keep questions of relevance to the fore, let us suppose that these measures do succeed and henceforth focus on the *ideal RCT*: one where no causally relevant differences obtain between the two groups other than the policy and its effects.

I.B.5.2 What RCTs Establish

Consider an RCT designed to test what effect, if any, treatment x has in producing outcome y. The standard result from an RCT is the so-called "*treatment effect*," T, across the individuals participating in the study (letting $Exp(\theta)$ represent the expectation of θ and $=_{df}$ mean "is equal by definition"):

$$T =_{df} Exp(y(i)\,|\,x(i) = X) - Exp(y(i)\,|\,x(i) = X')$$

where X is the value of the treatment in the treatment group and X' is its value in the control group.

Of what use is the treatment effect? Here we shall present an argument familiar in the evidence-based policy literature that shows the link between a positive result—a positive treatment effect—in an ideal RCT and the causal conclusion that the result supports. This conclusion, we shall see, is that the policy tested genuinely appears in the causal principle governing the production of the outcome in the experimental situation and that the support factors for it were there for some individuals in the study population; or, in language we use throughout this book, the conclusion that *the policy played a positive causal role* given this principle. It is important for our subsequent discussion that this, although elegantly arrived at, is *all* that it establishes. It is a different and difficult question how that fact can be given the status of evidence for an effectiveness conclusion.

RCT Argument

Following the discussion in I.B.3.1, suppose (Premise 1) that y in the study population is determined by a causal principle of form CP:

$$CP : y(i)\ c = a_1 + a_2 y_0(i) + a_3 b(i) x(i) + a_4 z(i)$$

The formula makes clear that, for any individual i, b not only determines in part whether x contributes to y at all for i but it also, along with a_3, controls how much a given value of x will contribute to y. From CP and the definition of T it follows that

$$T =_{df} Exp(y(i) \,|\, x(i) = X) - Exp(y(i) \,|\, x(i) = X') = Exp(a_2 y_0(i) \,|$$
$$x(i) = X) - Exp(a_2\ y_0(i) \,|\, x(i) = X')$$
$$+ Exp(a_3 b(i) \,|\, x(i) = X) X \quad Exp(a_3 b(i) \,|\, x(i) = X') X'$$
$$+ Exp(a_4 z(i) \,|\, x(i) = X) - Exp(a_4 z(i) \,|\, x(i)) = X').$$

If you are prepared to suppose (Premise 2) that the masking and random assignment of individuals to X and X' assures that for individuals in the study, x is probabilistically independent of y_0, b, and z, as it should be in the ideal, then

$$T = a_3 Exp(b(i))(X - X').$$

Conclusion. If T is positive then $a_3 b$ is also positive for at least some individuals. So x genuinely appears as a cause for y in the law CP for the study population. As we say, *x plays a positive causal role* under that principle. If $a_3 = 0$ or $b = 0$ for all individuals, then x does not appear in CP. So under CP, x makes no contribution to y outcomes for any individual, it plays no causal role; the outcomes for y are produced entirely by the quantities represented in the other three terms in CP.

Notice that the treatment effect averages across the b values for different individuals. This has two important consequences. First is the familiar fact that averages conceal what is happening to individuals. A positive treatment effect is perfectly consistent with x making substantial negative contributions to y for a great many individuals in the population. This is apparently what was happening with the teenage antidepressant that was helpful on average but seemed to make some of those treated with it suicidal (MHRA 2004). Second, although a positive treatment effect shows that b must be positive for at least some individuals, the reverse is not the case. A zero average is consistent with exceedingly high values of b, both positive and negative, for every individual. So a positive treatment effect shows that x can play a positive causal role anywhere the same causal principle obtains, but the lack of treatment effect does not show that x cannot play a causal role under that principle.

I.B.5.3 Alternatives to RCTs

RCTs are supposed to be the gold standard for evidence in evidence-based policy. Says who? That's the verdict of the usual evidence-ranking schemes recommended for evidence-based policy and used by most policy vetting agencies and policy warehouses. A good example is GRADE, constructed by the Grading of Recommendations Assessment, Development and Evaluation Working Group, which is used by over 50 organizations worldwide (Balshem et al. 2011). You can see their scheme, updated in 2011, in figure IV.3, along with the definitions of what the various ratings are supposed to mean, in table IV.1. Although RCTs are at the top there, better than RCTs, both in GRADE's overall philosophy and in most other ranking schemes, are meta-analyses of RCTs and systematic reviews. Why?

Meta-analyses

Many RCTs have small populations enrolled in the study. This threatens the validity of statistical inference. Suppose there's a difference between the number of positive outcomes in the treatment group versus the control group. That could reflect a genuine difference in outcome probabilities. Or, it could be just an accident, like getting 10 heads in a row in flipping a fair coin. The larger the population, the less likely this kind of statistical accident is. Meta-analyses use statistical techniques to blend together populations from different trials, tending carefully to differences between study designs, to create an imaginary super population in which inference from differences in frequencies of outcomes to differences in probabilities is more secure.

Systematic reviews

These are meant, in the words of the Campbell Collaboration, to "sum up the best available research on a specific question. This is done by synthesizing the results of several studies."[6] The studies need not all be RCTs. But they are meant to be "best available," that is, of high quality judged by some explicit, well-grounded criteria. The criteria are given in the evidence-ranking schemes. In our words, the results of the studies included in the review are meant to be highly trustworthy.

Often the reviewers start by looking at dozens, even hundreds, of studies but end up with only a handful that meet the inclusion criteria. This gives rise to some lively debate. Surely it is better, opponents argue, to base a synthetic judgment on all the studies available, taking into account the merits and defects of each. In particular, what if there were two or three high quality studies that pointed one way and a very great many others of varying lesser quality, with a variety of different merits and demerits, that point in the opposite direction? Surely in that case you should not have high confidence in a verdict based on just the few top quality studies. This fits with a standard doctrine about scientific confirmation, based on what is called the *no-miracles argument*.[7] It would be a miracle, so the argument goes, if so many separate, different kinds of defects from different kinds of studies conspired in just the right way to produce similar results. Unless, of course, there were some truth to those results.

Those who advocate considering only the most trustworthy results make two replies. First, "Garbage in, garbage out." Results that are not to be trusted taken as input produce untrustworthy results as output. Second, there's no well-grounded system for "weighing" up evidence of different kinds of different qualities. Too much must be left to judgment, and judgment is not to be trusted.

We do not want to join this argument. Whatever is the case about including less trustworthy results, it seems hard to quarrel with the idea that a verdict based on a synthesis of trustworthy results will be better than a verdict based on just this or that trustworthy result by itself. So, too, it seems hard to quarrel with the idea that a good meta-analysis of studies will be better than the verdict of a few smaller studies. That accounts for why these are at the top of the list.

But what about the study designs that appear below RCTs in the rankings? RCTs use Mill's method of difference as their underlying logic. In the GRADE list, "low" and "very low" quality studies do so as well, but without randomization. They are lower in rank because, without randomization, you are supposed to have less assurance that other causally relevant factors have the same distribution in treatment and control groups. Whether this risk is really high or low if you do not randomize, or you do not mask thoroughly at all possible places, depends on exactly what you know about other causal factors, which can sometimes be a lot and sometimes very little. Randomization is often defended by the claim that it is the only way to deal with unknown causal factors. If so, then an ideal RCT can be the superior choice if you are not very secure that you know much about what the significant causal factors are. Supposing that you are in this situation, then ranking good RCT studies above otherwise good studies that do not mask and randomize seems correct—so long as it is remembered as well that what is at stake is trustworthiness, not relevance or cost effectiveness or moral acceptability.

What's surprising, then, is not so much what is immediately above RCTs or immediately below, but what is left out of the usual lists altogether. An ideal RCT can *clinch* the result that the treatment works somewhere. We mean by this that if all the requirements for an ideal study are met, a difference in outcome probability between treatment and control groups deductively implies that the treatment caused the outcome in at least some individuals in the study population. That's what the RCT Argument of I.B.5.2 shows. But there's nothing special about RCTs in this regard. There are many methods where positive outcomes deductively imply causal conclusions, including certain kinds of econometric modeling, process tracing, and causal Bayes Nets methods. Each of these can establish causal conclusions reliably—provided the assumptions backing these study designs are met.

All methods require specific assumptions to be met if the conclusions drawn from them are to be justified. In particular, all methods establishing causal conclusions have assumptions about causality among their assumptions. Hence, the slogan, "no causes in; no causes out." All Mill's method-of-difference studies suppose, for example, that every probabilistic dependency has a causal explanation. And they suppose that all causes other than the treatment are distributed in the same way in the treatment and control groups. And they suppose that that means that, if treatment and outcome are probabilistically dependent in the study, there's no explanation left except that the treatment caused the effect in at least some individuals in the study. Other kinds of methods require other assumptions. We describe some of these here, very briefly, to acquaint you with them.

Causal Bayes Nets

These use probabilistic dependencies plus any available causal knowledge to infer new causal conclusions. Unlike RCTs, they do not need to suppose the probabilities are from an experimental situation; they can do with data from an ordinary nonexperimental population. Not surprisingly then, some of their assumptions are stronger than those required for RCTs. For example, they assume that, once information about a factor's causal predecessors has been taken into consideration, that factor will not be probabilistically dependent on anything except its own effects. Also, it is difficult to get many new results out without the additional assumption that the causally antecedent factors not taken into account are probabilistically independent of each other.[8]

Econometric methods

Econometrics has evolved a number of sophisticated techniques for using probabilities in nonexperimental populations to infer functional relations between factors that hold in those populations. But it is well known that not all true functional relations are causal. For instance, if causes are functionally related to their effects, then two effects of the same cause will be functionally related to each other even though neither causes the other. Sometimes, however, the genuine causal relations can be identified. This will be possible if an *instrumental variable* can be found. An instrumental variable is essentially one that affects the cause under test but none of the other possible causes of the putative effect.[9] It is also possible to identify genuine causal relations with other kinds of background causal information, though generally far more background information will be needed.[10]

Process tracing

This method confirms the existence of a causal connection between start and finish by confirming, one-by-one, a series of smaller causal steps in between. For the method to work, the steps in between must either be of a kind that are already well established or else be ones that can be established on the spot. Sometimes these intermediate steps are not established by direct observation but rather, for instance, by registering side effects that would be produced just in case the effect in question occurred, or by looking for effects of that effect. Process tracing is used regularly in daily life, often to draw negative conclusions. "My baseball couldn't be what broke your window since my baseball never went out of my backyard." And it is a familiar method in both biology and physics. It is also regularly used in post hoc policy evaluation. The Carvalho and White (2004) study of social funds, discussed in III.B.2.3, is a case in point.

All of these methods are reliable, so long as their requisite assumptions are met. That is, there are arguments just as rigorous as the RCT Argument to show that a causal conclusion follows deductively from positive results. The special advantage of RCTs seems to lie in the fact that few of their assumptions require knowledge about the factors that might be involved or their setting. We have invented the term "self-validating" to label this. In an RCT, you do not need to know a lot of background causal information about this factor or that since the basic assumptions are supposed to be justified by the design of the experiment itself. For instance, you do not have to know the other relevant causal factors to have reason to think they are distributed the same in the treatment and control groups. Randomization, masking, and placebo control are supposed to make this likely.

In many cases, however, there may well be enough information available to support reasonable confidence that assumptions for other methods are met; and in many cases it will be very difficult indeed to conduct a good RCT; and sometimes, as in the Nobel-prize winning work of James Heckman (Heckman and Vytlacil 2007), econometric methods can combine with randomized experiments to give better post hoc evaluations and predictions of policy success. So it is surprising that these other methods are not part of the evidence-based policy canon.

As with all other study designs, these kinds of studies can be done more or less well, and their background assumptions may be more or less trustworthy. They, like the study designs that appear in the usual evidence-ranking schemes, need vetting; and the vetting must be done by experts who know just what to look for. So knowing the existence of these methods is not likely to be of much realistic help to you in your attempts to use good evidence in your policy predictions until the social policy vetting agencies, warehouses, and systematic reviews figure out how to take them into account. In the meantime, much good evidence is being scattered to the winds.

I.B.6 RELEVANCE

I.B.6.1 What Makes RCT Results Relevant to Effectiveness Predictions?

This depends on the exact form of the effectiveness prediction. But before discussing that, it is important to notice that the treatment effect in an experimental population is not directly relevant to any effectiveness prediction outside the study population; its relevance will always be indirect. We shall for the most part discuss the weakest effectiveness prediction: "the policy will contribute positively if it is implemented here," where this will be determined under the causal principle that will hold here post-implementation. We focus on this, first, because it is the easiest to predict, requiring the fewest further assumptions, and, second, because, as we mentioned, you will need the same information, plus more, for any stronger predictions.

Start with the simplest case, where it can be taken for granted that the study situation and your situation—there and here—are subject to the same causal principle for the production of the targeted outcome y. Will x make the same average contribution; that is, is the efficacy, which is measured by the treatment effect in the study situation, the same there as here? Certainly if the same principle holds there as here, a_3 will be the same since it is constant. But $Exp(b(i))$ is not; it is an average—an average over x's support factors. The average in each situation depends on the distribution of these factors in that situation. Even if the same principles govern the two situations, that provides no reason to suppose that the distributions of support factors are the same. To the contrary, this distribution often depends heavily on local circumstances. So it is unlikely to be the same.

Moreover, the same distribution is not really what you hope for. What you would like is that you have or can arrange to have a distribution that favors the good values of b—the ones that provide the largest positive contribution from the policy. At the least, you will want to have some values that make x's contribution positive and these should outweigh the effects of those that make x's contribution negative; and if getting negative contributions in some individuals is to be avoided, then you don't want any of these "bad" values of b at all.

Laying aside for the moment worries about negative contributions in some individuals, suppose that you want to predict that the policy will contribute positively in your situation. What does it take to make RCT evidence relevant? Or, more broadly, since RCTs are only one way among many to support "it works somewhere," what does it take to make "it works there" (howsoever it is established) relevant to "it will work here"?

I.B.6.2 From "It Works There" to "It Works Here"

Suppose "it works somewhere" is trustworthy. When is that evidentially relevant to "it will work here" and under what conditions? From now on, we will take "it will work here" in its weakest sense. Unless we state otherwise,

"x works in situation S with respect to outcome y" means "x produces positive contributions to y for some individuals in S." Recall that this allows that x may produce negative contributions in other individuals, and may even produce an overall negative average contribution; and even if it produces an overall positive contribution on average, this does not mean that the average will be better than before because of the possible negative effects of other factors that change, either independently or as a result of implementing x.

When then will x work in S with respect to outcome y? That happens exactly when x genuinely appears in the causal principle that governs the production of y in S post-implementation and the support factors necessary for x to contribute to y are present for at least some individuals in S post-implementation. In the language we introduced earlier, when x *plays a positive causal role (with respect to y) in S.*

Now we are ready to address the question with which this section began. To know whether "it works somewhere" is evidentially relevant to "it will work here" and under what conditions, you have to start by asking what kind of argument can go from "it worked there" to "it will work here"? Here is one:

1. x works there (i.e., x genuinely appears in the causal principle that governs the production of y there post-implementation).
2. Here and there share that causal principle post-implementation.
3. The support factors necessary for x to contribute under that principle are present for at least some individuals here post-implementation.

Conclusion. x works here (i.e., x genuinely appears in the causal principle that governs the production of y here post-implementation and the support factors necessary for it to contribute to y are present for at least some individuals here post-implementation).

This argument reflects the fact that "it works there" gives information about the causal principle that obtains there and about the existence of the requisite support factors there. But it gives no information about what the causal principle here is nor about what support factors, if any, obtain here. You can think, "Surely it is the same here as there." Maybe so. But the issue is: "What do you have warrant for; what degree of confidence are you justified in?" not "What do you think?" And the answer to the question, "The same how?" matters. Heedful of our remarks in I.B.6.1 about the distribution of support factors, this argument does not suppose the distributions to be the same in both locations. The argument would be valid—the conclusion would still follow from the premises—with that premise substituted for premise 3. But the same distribution is not necessary for the conclusion that it will work for some individuals here; and, as we noted, a "better" distribution here than there would be preferable.

This argument nevertheless demands a lot. It requires the same causal principle to govern the production of the outcome here as there. Recall that a causal principle records the full set of causes that operate, what each contributes, and how they combine. That's what it takes for nature to set the value the outcome will have. But in many domains the causes that operate shift frequently and unpredictably, from locale to locale and from time to time, as economists from John Stuart Mill ([1836] 1967, [1843] 1850: bk. VI) to British econometrician David Hendry (Hendry and Mizon 2011) have argued. That's why, said Mill, economics cannot be an inductive science. The principles that held in the past can in no way be relied on to hold in the future, due to the shifting of causes.

But that need not make information about causes there irrelevant to what happens anywhere else. As Mill stressed, many causes have what he called a "stable tendency." They make the same contribution across a variety of different situations; that is, they appear in the same form across a variety of different principles. The forces of physics are a clear example. In different situations—from Galileo dropping balls from the Leaning Tower to airplanes flying at 10,000 feet above the Earth to electrons moving in a battery—gravity always makes a contribution (the same contribution) to the total force exerted on the object, a contribution of size GMm/r^2. It does so no matter what other causes affect the outcome; it *plays the same causal role* in all the different causal principles for all the different situations where masses appear.

Not all causes have stable tendencies. Some seem to operate totally locally. Among those that do have stable tendencies, the range of stability can vary. Perhaps some are universally stable, but most have boundaries. They make the same contribution in a range of situations but not in others, where the breadth of the range can vary dramatically. The trick is to figure out what kinds situations are safely within the range. Within that range you can suppose that the contribution you see there will appear here as well. Ideally this is what science will provide for you. But often the science has not done so, or not done so yet, especially with the kinds of causes at stake in social, economic, and health policy. Then you will have to think about this—seriously—for your special situation and get what advice and help you can.

Chapter II.B is all about finding the right kind of causes to be employed in policy design, ones that can make a positive contribution in your setting. A policy that is known to have a stable tendency to contribute positively will fit the bill perfectly. But warranting assumptions about stability of contribution is difficult—it is the meat of serious ongoing science. Nevertheless you may have to rely on assumptions like these being true if your policy is to work. For very often the best warrant for the claim that x plays a causal role here is that it is already well established that x has a stable tendency to produce y, stable across a wide variety of kinds of situations, including ones like yours. It produces a positive contribution to y in some individuals here because it always—across this range—produces a positive contribution for some individuals, or, even possibly for all individuals. So watch out. This is a difficult assumption to warrant and where the warrant for it is weak, so too is the warrant for any effectiveness predictions it is supposed to support.

We shall, for shorthand, say *x can play a causal role with respect to outcome y* in a situation if x genuinely appears in the causal principles for that situation. For principles of form CP, that means that *x does* (or *will*) *play a causal role in situation S* if it can play a causal role under the principles that govern S and the support factors (designated by b) required under those principles take nonzero values for some individuals. Then *x can play the same causal role in situation S' as in S* means that it genuinely appears in the principles for the situation S just in case it genuinely appears in those governing situation S' and with the same sign. This is difficult knowledge to come by.

Even if you are reasonably warranted in the assumption that the policy can play a positive causal role in your situation, it is essential to keep in mind that a policy can play both a positive causal role for some individuals and a negative role for others. If this matters, you had better be at pains to learn about both possibilities. And, recall, to predict which dominates, you will need information about the distribution of values of the support factors for the positive and negative roles.

A final thing to note is that it is generally a whole causal team that has a stable tendency, not an individual cause by itself. Recall, individual causes are generally INUS conditions. Each is usually only part of what it takes to get a contribution. It seems that usually, where there are stable tendencies, the entire team is required to get the stable contribution. Masses, like the sun, cause other masses, like the planets, to experience an attractive force. But what that force is depends not just on the first mass alone (the mass of the sun)—that is only an INUS cause—but on the whole team, which includes the constant of gravity (which is an instance of what we have called a "boost factor"), the mass of the second body (the planet), and the separation between them. You won't get the stable contribution to the force if any member of the team fails to show up for work.

With these considerations in mind, we can construct a different argument for getting from "it works there" to "it will work here," one that does not require the same causal principle to obtain here and there but substitutes for this the assumption that the policy *plays the same causal role* here as there.

Effectiveness Argument

1. x played a positive causal role there.

2. x can play the same causal role here post-implementation as there.

3. The support factors necessary for x to play a positive causal role here are present for at least some individuals here post-implementation.

Conclusion. x works here (i.e., x can play a positive causal role here post-implementation and the support factors necessary for it to do so are present for at least some individuals here post-implementation).

Our task in this section has been to show how to get from results that provide good evidence for "it works there" to the conclusion "it will work here." The task is almost accomplished. All that's needed is to add, as support under the Effectiveness Argument, a sub-subargument, like the RCT Argument of section I.B.5.2, that takes the study results as one of its premises and that concludes with "x plays a positive causal role there." If you find the policy vetted by a good policy warehouse like What Works or the Campbell Collaboration, you can take for granted that there is a good argument like this for premise (1). With this addition, the Effectiveness Argument does the job.

This Effectiveness Argument is the one we shall rely on throughout. That's because it is a very special argument. Not only do its premises imply its conclusion, as they should in any good argument. In addition, its premises are necessary for the conclusion; the conclusion will not hold without them. Suppose, as we have been taking for granted about the policy under consideration, that it has been shown to work there, say in an RCT study. If the policy does not play the same causal role here as there, it will not work here. Similarly, if the necessary support factors for it are not in place here post-implementation, it will not work here. So for the policy to succeed here, premises (2) and (3) must be true. If they are not true, the policy will definitely not work here.

I.B.6.3 External Validity

This is a central notion in the RCT orthodoxy, and it does not do the job that it is meant to do. It is meant to deal with the issue that we have raised, whether a policy that has been shown to have worked by a good study can be expected to work in a different context. Every practical person knows, from the high risks and failure often found in rolling out successful pilots, that this is a real problem. So it has to be faced. That's what this book is about.

The orthodoxy approaches this by distinguishing between *internal validity* and *external validity*. A study has *internal validity* when the study provides strong warrant for the study results. The RCT Argument of I.B.5.2 shows that RCTs can provide strong warrant for causal conclusions. There are well-established procedures, to do with randomization, masking, and so on, for ensuring that a positive treatment effect—a positive average difference between what happens to those who had the treatment, say a drug or small classes, and those who did not—implies that the treatment played a role in producing the outcome in the study population. We have no quarrel with this or generally with the notion of internal validity. We think that there are many well-conducted RCTs, that many are internally valid, and that the casual conclusions that they show are trustworthy.

In the orthodoxy, a study has *external validity* when the "same treatment" has the "same result" in a specific target as it did in the study. The orthodox advice is that external validity can be expected if the target population is "sufficiently similar" to the study population. For us, the key question is how good a job this advice does in getting you from "it worked there" to "it will work here." The answer: you are lucky if it gets you anywhere. First, the advice is vague, surprisingly so given how specific the orthodox guidelines are in assessing RCTs, meta-analyses, and systematic reviews. Second, similarity, if taken seriously, is too demanding; you'd hardly ever be able to export study results if you insisted on similarity. Third, similarity is the wrong idea anyway. Fourth, it is wasteful.

First, *the advice is vague.* "Same treatment." Using the same treatment can be fine—so long as you have identified the right description for the treatment. And the right description is the one that plays the same causal role in the target as in the study. Recall our illustration in I.B.3.2. For Bangladesh and Tamil Nadu, that's "educate the person in power," not "educate the mother."

"Same result." What result? Suppose you are interested in getting the "same treatment effect." This won't happen unless the policy can play the same causal role in the two populations. Let's make that easy by supposing that the two populations are governed by the same causal principle, say a principle of form CP in I.B.3.1. Recall from the RCT Argument that the treatment effect in a population depends on the average of $b(i)$ there. In this case $b(i)$ represents in one fell swoop all the different support factors necessary in the population if the policy is to produce a contribution there. Each separate combination of values of these factors corresponds to a different value of $b(i)$. The treatment effect depends on the average of these values across the study population. Averages depend on the probabilities for the numbers averaged over; so, the treatment effect depends on the probabilities for each different arrangement of values of the support factors, where each different arrangement is represented by a different value, B, for $b(i)$: $Prob(b(i) = B)$.

So, when can you expect the average of $b(i)$ to be the same in the two populations? Represent the probabilities in the two by $Prob_{SP}$ for the study population and $Prob_{TP}$ for the target population. You can expect the average to be the same when

$$Prob_{SP}(b(i) = B) = Prob_{TP}(b(i) = B)$$

for all B's; that is, when all the combinations of values of the support factors have the same probability in the study and target populations. Otherwise, it is an accident of the numbers.

So, except for lucky accidents, the treatment effect will be the same in the study and the target only if the policy can play the same causal role in the two populations, the support factors are the same, and the distribution of their values is the same in the two populations. That's a tall order indeed. It is an absurdly tough test to require the same treatment effect as in the study population. If that then is external validity, there is no real chance that a study will have it.

But perhaps "same effect" is to be understood differently. Maybe as "same overall outcome"; or, "same in making a positive contribution in both places." These are different predictions, and, as in I.B.4, different kinds of facts must be in place for these different predictions to come true. It's these facts you need to know about if you want to predict that you'll get the "same result," not some vague set of similarities.

What about similarity? In what ways are the target and the study to be similar? In all the ways you can think of? Maybe you don't need to bother getting more precise about what similarity means, though, because of our second and third worries.

Second, *similarity is too demanding.* Consider a paper by a team of authors from Chicago, Harvard, and Brookings, "What Can We Learn about Neighborhood Effects from the Moving to Opportunity Experiment?" (Ludwig et al. 2008). The paper explicitly addresses the question of where outside the experimental population you are entitled to suppose the experimental results will obtain—for instance, where can you expect higher high school graduation rates for girls in the families that moved. The authors first report "MTO defined its eligible sample as . . ." We won't write out their long list in this quotation because you can read it in their conclusion:

Thus MTO data . . . are strictly informative only about this population subset—people residing in high-rise public housing in the mid-1990's, who were at least somewhat interested in moving and sufficiently organized to take note of the opportunity and complete an application. The MTO results should only be extrapolated to other populations if the other families, their residential environments, and their motivations for moving are similar to those of the MTO population. (Ludwig et al. 2008: 154–55)

If that's the limit of where MTO results are relevant, maybe it wasn't worth doing the study in the first place.

Third, *similarity is the wrong idea.* Consider the list in the MTO quote. It's a potpourri. The authors seem to have tossed in everything they could think of without system or reason; why for instance did they leave out the geographical location of the cities in the experiment? And anyway, the list does not get at what is necessary. Look at it again. You know that the same treatment effect requires that the policy play the same causal role in the two populations and the support factors have the same distribution in both. Are we really meant to suppose that sharing this long list of factors will ensure that?

Maybe you are to think of the factors in this list just as indicators, where the hope is that sharing the indicators ensures that the two populations share the facts that really matter. But why are these good indicators? If you offer a list of indicators, you need some defense of why the indicators are up to the job. And this will be hard to give without any thought about how MTO plays the role it did in the Chicago study population and of what its support factors might be here.

We are not alone in our demands that you must try explicitly to identify the support factors. Here is what Edward Leamer, an econometrician famous for a classic paper, "Taking the Con out of Econometrics," has to say about it, using slightly different language (his "confounders" are our "support factors"):

. . . the overall treatment effect is not a number but a variable that depends on the confounding effects. . . . If little thought has gone into identifying these possible confounders, it seems probable that little thought will be given to the limited applicability of the results in other settings.

. . . which is a little like the lawyer who explained that when he was a young man he lost many cases he should have won but as he grew older he won many that he should have lost, so that on the average justice was done. (Leamer 2010: 35–36)

Fourth, *similarity is wasteful.* The treatment effect averages over arrangements for the support factors. Some of these arrangements enable the policy to make a big contribution, others only a small contribution. And for others the policy may even be counterproductive. You shouldn't aim for the *same* mix of these arrangements in your population as in the study population. Rather you want a *good* mix—a mix that concentrates on arrangements that allow the policy to do the most for you.

We have been talking mostly about expecting the same treatment effect. That, we said, is a tall order. Why not drop the hope that the policy will produce the same treatment effect and substitute something weaker, like "it will make a positive contribution" or "it will produce an improvement over what would have happened otherwise." Should you be looking for similarities between your population and the study population in these cases? No. You should be looking for what matters to getting the prediction you have in view right. What's wrong with the ideas of external validity and similarity is that they invite you to stop thinking. Why did you decide to try it in Bangladesh? Presumably because you thought that it might work there. Why? Presumably because you had some idea of how and why the policy might work. And that, using our categories, is about causal roles and support factors. Only by thinking in terms of causal roles and support factors can you begin to see what evidence you need if you are going to bet that the policy will work here. You cannot avoid thinking like that. The notions of external validity and similarity are no substitutes.

I.B.7 BOTTOM LINE, PUT SIMPLY

I.B.7.1 Introduction and Apologia

This section aims to give you a simplified version of our theory, so that you can read the rest of the book even if the theory chapter so far has left you confused. As with all simplifications, we cannot pretend that it contains all the detail and rigor of the full version. And it simplifies by, among other things, making what we say rather cruder, so that the skeleton of the analysis is visible without so many qualifications and complexities. This is at a cost, so that even the previously confused reader may wonder at times whether our assertions here can properly be as bald as they are. But that is for clarity.

And in the rest of the book we use the theory to back our discussion. That discussion will inevitably use more or less technical terms, and most of those appear in this section *italicized*. But we have also tried to use simpler language that relies on the theory without always making it rigorously explicit. That too is not without cost. But it may further encourage those who find our theory hard.

I.B.7.2 How Our Theory Works

This book is about evidence, because it is about evidence-based policy. The point of evidence-based policy is to choose policies that are effective, that will work. And that means will work where and when they are put into effect—what we call *here*. And the general question is, what kind of evidence, and in any particular case, exactly what evidence, will help you with that *effectiveness prediction*. To start to answer that, we need to step back. We need to think about causes and effects and we need to think about evidence.

Will this policy work here, in your setting? Will it cause the result you want where you are? That depends on what the *causal principles* are where you are. Causal principles fix what causes what. Your policy will not produce the outcome you want if there's no causal principle connecting the two. Getting lung cancer is correlated with owning ashtrays. But buying ashtrays will not bring on lung cancer. There's a causal principle, studied in the biomedical sciences, that connects smoking and lung cancer; and there's a causal principle, studied by sociologists and market researchers, that connects smoking and owning ashtrays. But there's no casual principle that connects buying ashtrays and lung cancer.

The causal principles that hold where you are fix two important facts that matter to whether your policy will work here. The first is about *causal roles*: Can the policy play a role in producing the desired outcome in your setting? Smoking can play a causal role in producing lung cancer; owning an ashtray can't. The second is about support factors: What other factors must be in place for it to do so? Maybe smoking only produces lung cancer if one has the right genes. But genes or not, there's no way ashtrays will play a role in producing lung cancer. There's no support factors that can help.

Turn to evidence now. You are looking for evidence to support an effectiveness prediction, a prediction that your policy will work here, where you are. The facts that you need to support this prediction cannot be just any old facts—it is Thursday. They have to be relevant facts. That is what evidence is. It is evidence for something. In this case, for a conclusion that is an *effectiveness prediction*.

And conclusions are the result of *arguments*. That is a technical term. It does not mean, for example, "reason" as in "my argument for going was that I had promised to." It means a chain of reasoning, or more strictly a set of claims—premises—set out in support of a conclusion. The familiar syllogism *"All men are mortal. Socrates is a man. Therefore Socrates is mortal"* is an argument in which *Socrates is a man* is relevant and therefore, if a fact, evidence by virtue of playing a role in the argument that leads to the conclusion. "It is Thursday" plays no such role.

So to make an *effectiveness prediction* you need to know what facts to verify. They have to be the facts relevant to the prediction—that is what makes them evidence. What is relevant is determined by the structure of the *argument*, the chain of reasoning, that leads to the prediction. Because that *argument* is about what causes the outcome in your setting, its structure will reflect facts about the *causal principles* that hold there, in particular, facts about *causal roles* and *support factors*.

Having promised simplicity, we may in the last paragraph have delivered only brevity without clarity. So in the rest of this section, we use some of the analysis from the earlier parts of the chapter to put (back) some of the flesh on the bones of the discussion. But before that, two further points.

We say that "you need to know what facts to verify." Our book tries to help with that question. But it does not tell you how to verify the facts you need once you have identified them. The distinction is important. If you want to drive off by pressing the accelerator, you rely on a causal principle in which the presence of fuel plays a causal role. We help you to realize that, therefore, *there is fuel* is relevant, and that you need evidence for it. We do not help with how you find out whether there is fuel, how you get that evidence. In this toy example, finding out is trivial—look at the fuel gauge or dip the tank. Often it is not trivial. At worst, it may not even be clear how you would verify some facts. But anyway, we do not deal with that. And the main reason is that there are a very large number of ways of establishing facts, and hence evidence, from common observation to elaborate statistical research.

Second, we spend time here using our theory of evidence to discuss what is the relevance of the fact that a good RCT has shown that the policy worked there. We show that, although this may indeed be a fact, whether it is relevant, and hence evidence, depends on what *argument* it contributes to. And it turns out that its relevance will often be slight.

I.B.7.3 Causal Principles

"Will this policy work here?" The question focuses attention on the policy. But to answer it, your focus must be directed elsewhere. Where? The answer to that is supplied by considering some general facts about how causes work to produce their effects.

Causes do not produce their effects willy-nilly but for a reason. They produce effects in some systematic way, in accord with some causal principles. A causal principle for a situation lays out all the factors that operate to bring about the outcome in question in that situation and shows how these combine to produce it. We stress three important facts about causal principles that matter to getting the right prediction about whether a proposed policy will work for you:

1. The causal principles that underwrite policy prediction are not universal.
2. Few causes work on their own; causal factors work together in teams.
3. There are generally a number of distinct teams at work in any situation, each making its own contribution to the effect.

1. *Causal principles are not universal.* They differ from place to place and from time to time. That means that it is not enough for you to know that the policy worked somewhere or even that it has worked at some time here. "It worked there"; it played a positive causal role there. So it was one of the factors from a causal principle that holds there. To predict that it will work here, you need to know that it is one of the factors from a causal principle that holds here. That is what ensures that it can play a positive causal role for you. You will read more about finding factors that can do so in II.B.

2. *Causes work in teams.* What gets highlighted as the *cause*—where for you that means your policy—is rarely enough to produce a contribution to the effect on its own. It needs team support. If any of the essential team members is absent, the policy won't make any contribution at all. It is like trying to make pancakes with no baking powder. So even if you know, maybe from a good RCT, that the policy worked there and that the same causal principles hold here as there, that is not enough to conclude that it will work here. That only shows that it *can* play a causal role here. To know that it *will* play a positive causal role here, you also need to know that you will have the requisite support factors here when you need them. That's what II.A is about.

3. *Distinct teams produce distinct contributions.* The overall effect achieved is usually made up of separate *contributions* from a number of different teams of causes, some of which can pull in different directions. The magnet, in team with the iron in the pin, contributes an upward force on the pin; the pull of the earth, in team with the pin's mass, contributes a downward force. The overall force is a combination of the two. Social causes are just the same. Some improve the outcome in view; others contribute negatively to it. This makes predicting the actual outcome difficult. To predict that, you must take account of all the factors at work and of how they combine; that is, you need to know the full causal principle.

Our concern is with less ambitious predictions than "What will the actual outcome be?" We focus on "Will this policy make a positive contribution?" Will it make things better for some individuals than they otherwise would be? In our terminology, "Will the policy *play a positive causal role* here?"

We talk more about the effects of other teams, both ones that do and ones that do not include the policy, in II.A.

I.B.7.4 Evidence, Argument, and Warrant

No one can doubt that basing your predictions about policy effectiveness on evidence is a good idea. But what counts as evidence—good evidence—that a policy worked there or that it will work here? Our answer is theory-based. It is grounded in a systematic account of evidence, knowledge, and warrant.

Some claims are self-evident or already well established. They do not need to be backed up by anything further for you to be justified in taking them to be true. Policy effectiveness predictions are not like that. They need support. What does the support look like? To justify having a high degree of confidence in a questionable claim, a claim that is not self-evident, you need to produce some further claims that, taken together, ensure that the questionable claim is likely to be true. That is, you need a good argument. An *argument*, recall, is a set of claims—premises—offered in support of a conclusion. A *good argument* is one in which the premises themselves are all well warranted—trustworthy—and together imply the conclusion, or at least make it highly likely. (In technical language, the first means that the argument is *sound*; the second, that it is *valid*.)

What holds in general holds for the particular case of policy effectiveness conclusions. There is nothing special about them in this respect. Suppose, then, you have trustworthy information that a policy works somewhere, or in a number of somewheres. So you can take for granted "it works there." What does it take for this information to count as evidence for "it will work here"? It takes a good argument, an argument in which the conclusion—"it will work here"—genuinely follows from the premises, including the premise "it works there," and the premises themselves are trustworthy. It is important to keep in mind that the conclusion of an argument can be no more trustworthy than any of its premises: dicey premises yield dicey conclusions. So identifying what all the premises are matters.

What then about evidence? Suppose you had access to a gigantic encyclopedia that reported every true fact there is. Which facts should get labeled "evidence for my conclusion" and which not? Evidence is supposed to help justify taking your conclusion to be true, and what it takes to do that is a good argument. So facts can't be just labeled "evidence for this conclusion" one way or another. It takes a good argument to connect the two. Any fact that gets so labeled will have to be one among many, possibly very many, premises that are each themselves well warranted and that together make the conclusion probable. This makes evidence highly conditional. No matter how trustworthy a fact from the encyclopedia or a result from a scientific study is, it provides no justification at all without the other premises to connect it to the conclusion.

I.B.7.5 Arguments for Effectiveness

For evidence-based policy you are urged to use only policies that have been shown to work somewhere. If you are lucky you will be able to find lists of such policies in a warehouse that vets studies and ensures that the claim "it works somewhere" is trustworthy. What does it take to turn that into evidence that it will work here? A good argument that takes "it works somewhere" as a premise and concludes with "it will work here."

There are a number of different arguments that can do the job, with more and less demanding premises. The Effectiveness Argument from I.B.6.2 is the argument of choice for evidence-based policy. It has the weakest premises and, what really matters, its premises are essential to the truth of the conclusion. If either premise (2) or premise (3) of this argument is false, the policy that worked there will not work here. We express this argument in a very simple, straightforward form here.

The basic argument that links "it worked there" with effectiveness predictions looks like this:

Effectiveness Argument

1. The policy worked there (i.e., it played a positive causal role in the causal principles that hold there and the support factors necessary for it to play this positive role there were present for at least some individuals there).

2. The policy can play the *same causal role* here as there.

3. The *support factors* necessary for the policy to play a positive causal role here are in place for at least some individuals here post-implementation.

Conclusion. The policy will work here.

By support factors, we mean the other members of the team of causes that will be required for the policy to make a contribution. Of course it is going to be difficult to warrant a claim like premise (3) without any commitment about what the support factors are. So you will probably have to have a subargument that defends your claims about what these factors are in your situation.

So there are two further pieces of information besides "it works there" that are needed to justify taking "it will work here" as true. These are our chief focus in this book. We explain about them in detail, and with examples: the first, which concerns causal roles, in II.B and the second, which concerns support factors, in II.A. In III we provide advice for how to go about identifying the information these premises demand.

Our central claim in this book is made graphic in figures I.5 and I.6. If you start, as you are urged to do, with evidence that the policy you are considering worked somewhere, the prediction that the same policy will work here, in your situation, is like the seat of a three-legged stool. It doesn't matter how sturdy one leg is, if either of the others fails, the stool collapses and you are dumped flat on the ground.

Figure I.5: A well-supported effectiveness prediction

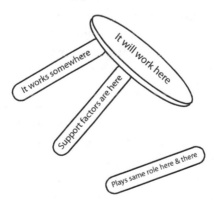

Figure I.6: What happens when a premise is missing

I.B.7.6 RCTs and Effectiveness Predictions

Randomized controlled trials (RCTs) are supposed to be the gold standard in evidence-based policy. So we want now to apply our theory to the claim that a good RCT is strong evidence for an effectiveness claim.

A good RCT with a positive outcome does indeed show that the policy worked somewhere; that it made a positive contribution for some individuals there, then, in the study population under the study conditions. In our language, "it played a positive causal role there." That tells you something about the causal principles that obtained there. It guarantees that the policy appears in a team that contributes positively according to those principles and that all the other members of the team—the *support factors*—were present there for at least some individuals in the study population.

That information is not much use to you if, as we discuss in II.B, the causal principles for your situation are very different from those of the study situation. So, to use this RCT result to back up a prediction that the policy will work here in your situation—that it will play a positive causal role here—you need warrant for assuming that the principles that hold here are sufficiently like those that hold there. They do not need to be exactly the same. You may have a different mix of causal factors at work. But they definitely must be the same in this respect: the policy appears in both principles and in a team whose contribution is positive. Whatever is true about what other causes you have here and whatever they have there, if the policy is to make a positive contribution here, it must appear in the principles here just as it did in the principles there.

If the principles are the same in this respect, we say that the policy *could* play a positive causal role here. We say "could" for a good reason. Whether it will or not depends on whether you will have here all the other members of the team needed to support it according to the causal principles that obtain here, and at the right times. If you know that's the case, you can predict with high confidence that the policy will play a positive casual role here just as it did in the RCT.

So a positive outcome in an RCT shows that the putative cause *did play* a causal role in the study situation. It did so because it *could* play a positive role there—it appears in a team that makes a positive contribution under the causal principles that hold there; and because, for some individuals in that situation, the support factors for it were in place. That's what we mean by "*It worked there*"—there, in the study population. Hence, "*It works somewhere.*"

There is also the case where it *could play* a causal role but does not because not all the factors in the support team are present. We want to make this distinction between *did play* and *could play* to preserve the insight that an intervention may have the potential to play a causal role in producing an outcome, even if it does not because not all the support factors are present. So small class sizes *could* play a causal role in producing better reading scores in California, even if that policy did not play a causal role because there were not enough good teachers to take the larger number of classes. *Could* then refers to the fact that smaller class sizes did at least figure as part of the causal principles, that is, as part of a story about relevant factors and how they combine to produce the effect. Unlike eating tomatoes twice a day, which does not figure as a part of a causal principle for reading scores, so forget support factors.

To turn RCT results into evidence it takes a good argument—an argument with trustworthy premises from which the conclusion genuinely follows. We have proposed above in I.B.7.5 an argument—the Effectiveness Argument—that gets you to the conclusion you want, that the policy will work here. But you can see that RCT results do not figure anywhere in this argument. Where do they enter? They figure as a premise in a subargument—the RCT Argument—for a premise in the Effectiveness Argument, as in figure I.7.

The RCT Argument (which we described in I.B.5.2) starts with the claim that the results were positive in the study and concludes that the policy played a positive causal role there—"it worked there." The other premises in the RCT Argument describe the design of the study and provide the connection between causes and probabilities that allows a causal conclusion to be derived from a difference in the average values of the outcome in the treatment and control groups.

We do not focus on the RCT Argument, since there are a number of good warehouses, like What Works and the Campbell Collaboration, that take on the job of policing RCT Arguments for you. Although they may not put it this way, what they do is to check to make sure, for specific studies, that the other premises in the RCT Argument are trustworthy, so that a positive result in the study does indeed support the claim that the policy played a positive causal role there. What we are concerned with are all the things that have to be established once the RCT Argument is in place—the other premises in the Effectiveness Argument. This is what our lessons are about.

The important lesson about RCTs is that the relevance of RCT results is highly conditional, depending on both the Effectiveness Argument and the RCT Argument.

As in figure I.7, a positive result in an RCT is leveraged into evidence that "it works there," there in the RCT situation, by the RCT Argument. Then "it works there" is leveraged into evidence for "it works here" by the Effectiveness Argument. If either of these arguments fails, as in figure I.8, the lever drops. The evidential relevance disappears with a thud. Worse, you will end up with a policy that does not work for you.

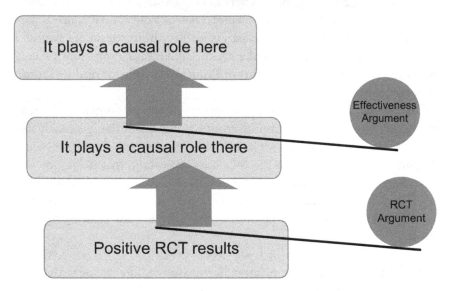

Figure I.7: The RCT as *conditional evidence* for effectiveness

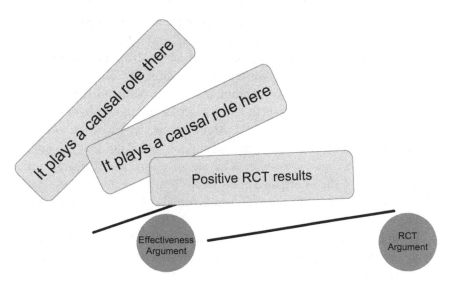

Figure I.8: When the argument fails

PART TWO

Paving the Road from "There" to "Here"

CHAPTER II.A

Support Factors

Causal Cakes and Their Ingredients

II.A.1 WHERE WE ARE AND WHERE WE ARE GOING

The last section of the theory chapter, I.B.7, gives you all you need for the rest of the book, even if you did not read the whole of that chapter. But to understand that much is important. As we have said before, we need theory because we want to show that our ideas about predicting policy effectiveness are principled. Our advice is rooted in a theory, a theory of *evidence for use*. This is a theory designed specifically for the user's problem of understanding what kinds of knowledge are good for reliable predictions about whether policies will work for you as you would implement them.

Our theory implies that to move from "it worked somewhere" to "it will work here" you will have to worry about *support factors*. You will need, we said, to have evidence about what are the support factors that must be in place if your policy is to produce a contribution and you will need evidence that these factors will actually obtain in your setting.

In this section we want to explain what support factors are and why they are so important. We begin with a simple, familiar example and an easy framework within which to picture them. It does not require the same language as the theory, but you will see that it nevertheless reflects our theoretical requirements. Looking for these support factors is what we call *horizontal search*. That is by contrast with vertical search, which is the topic of II.B.

II.A.2 READING SCORES: A CASE STUDY

Suppose that you want to improve reading scores, and that you are considering a policy of introducing homework to achieve that. What follows here is a framework for thinking about how, if it were to work, it might work. We shall take it for granted for the moment that homework can play a causal role in improving reading scores for your students. But what will it take to ensure it does so?

Our framework for thinking about the causal role of a policy depends on the notion of a *cake*. (We focus on the cake representation because it is graphic and because it makes vivid our central messages. But see Appendix I for a discussion of other ways of representing how causes produce their effects.) Figure II.1 is a possible cake for homework and reading test scores (Cooper, Robinson, and Patall 2006).

This is how you read the cake. It tells what has to be in place if homework is to contribute to higher test scores. It says that for that contribution you need all of:

- Student ability
- Study space
- Student motivation
- Homework
- Consistent lessons
- Supportive family
- Work feedback
- Other

The cake is just a picture of the list. In our theoretical language, the other ingredients in the cake are *support factors* necessary if homework is actually to play a causal role in improving reading scores.

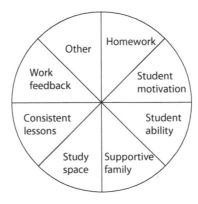

Figure II.1: A cake for improved reading scores

The cake metaphor is, we hope, a useful way of visualizing what we have to say in our theory about what you need to know to predict that a policy will work here in your situation. It may look informal, and it is certainly meant to be friendlier than the list. But it achieves that without loss of rigor. You can use the language of the list to talk about what the cake shows. The policy is one ingredient in the cake, and it plays its causal role by working with the other ingredients, its support factors, to produce a contribution to the effect.

Epidemiologists sometimes use the term "pie" instead of "cake" and talk about slices. We prefer "cakes" and "ingredients" to underline that each ingredient is necessary. If you take a slice out of a pie, you still have a lot of pie left. But if you take away a basic ingredient in a cake, you don't get the right cake at all. That is just what is supposed to be the case with the support factors for the policy. Without them you just do not get the expected contribution.[1]

Note that we say "contribution." Ensuring you have a whole cake present cannot of itself fix the value of the effect—reading scores—that will appear. Why? Because this cake, with its contribution, is only one of many that may be around in your situation. Suppose that activating this cake by introducing homework will contribute an improvement. Then introducing this new good contribution from the cake that includes the homework must at least make things better than it would have been without the homework—supposing nothing else changes as well. Suppose even that you know the size of the contribution of that cake (a big assumption). Then you will know what it adds to the value of the effect. But you won't know what that actual value is since that depends on what other cakes are at work too. To estimate what the actual values are, you need to represent more cakes—all the cakes that can make a contribution to reading scores. That's what we discuss in the next section.

II.A.3 INUS CONDITIONS

Another way of talking about cakes and ingredients is in terms of the philosopher's notion of *INUS conditions*. What's an INUS condition? An INUS condition is an Insufficient but Necessary part of an Unnecessary but Sufficient condition for getting a contribution to the effect you want.

Start with the second half of the definition. The cake, as pictured above, is sufficient—it is enough—to produce a positive contribution. If you have that cake, you get a contribution to better reading scores. But it is commonplace that there is more than one way to skin a cat. A contribution to the effect can always be generated from a variety of different cakes with different ingredients. Each particular cake is Unnecessary for getting a contribution to the effect, since you can get contributions, both positive and negative, from lots of alternative cakes. For instance there are many ways to contribute to improving reading scores that do not involve homework at all, like getting parents more involved, especially in reading to children at home, or connecting the reading with something the children want to do independently, like cooking from recipes or finding their way on their own on the subway. But it is Sufficient to produce that contribution. If a bundle—or *team*—of factors, a cake, is sufficient that just means that they are enough, that you don't need to add any more to get a contribution.

Now for the INUS conditions. An INUS condition is an ingredient, a part of the cake. By itself it is an Insufficient part—it is not enough on its own to produce a contribution. It needs the other ingredients as support factors. You only get a contribution from the cake if you have all the support factors. But it is Necessary, meaning if you are going to get that contribution to better scores from that cake, you have to have that factor present in the cake.

Thinking about policy is complicated and has to avoid (at least) two traps. The first is betting on the policy without:

1. Thinking what support factors have to be present if it is to make a contribution.

And even if you don't fall into that trap you may well have very false expectations about what scores you will actually see in the end if you proceed without:

2. Thinking what other cakes may be making contributions, including, but not only, from the introduction of your policy.

In our language, to predict what will actually happen you have both to look at the ingredients in the cake that contains your policy and also to think about what other cakes may be making contributions, good or bad. This kind of thinking is what we call *horizontal search*. For the most part, though, predicting what will actually happen is way beyond your means, since you generally will have little knowledge of what other cakes will be operating. So mostly our advice is geared to helping you predict not what will actually happen all told, but at least whether your proposed policy will make things better.

II.A.4 BETTER READING SCORES

How do INUS conditions help you to think about the failure of the California experiment with smaller classes to achieve better reading scores? Two factors stand out in the ex post analysis of why the California program did not achieve its intended results—availability of space and of good teachers.

In Tennessee, the project involved only schools that had available space. In California, there was often not enough spare space. So sometimes space was found, but it was not as good as existing classrooms. And it was taken away from other activities that might be thought important for student achievement—special needs, music and arts, athletics, and child care programs. Second, Tennessee had no shortage of qualified teachers to staff the reduced size classes. But California had to hire an additional 12,000 teachers. And many of these were unqualified.

This analysis illustrates the need for horizontal search to identify what the requisite support factors are when you consider how you are going to implement the policy. The program in California was rolled out statewide over the course of a year. Within a very short time class sizes were cut in half. Both the problems in California were brought on by the very large scale of the implementation there and its speed. The large scale meant that there was little chance of mimicking Tennessee in these two important ways. California did not limit the policy to schools with space and spare teachers. And it did not allow the system time to adjust and create the extra teachers and space needed.

Put that in terms of a single cake and its INUS conditions. Small classes is the policy variable, and it is one ingredient in the cake. Improved student achievement is the desired contribution. What are the other factors, the support team, with which California should have filled out the cake before it started? The post-program evaluation shows that properly qualified teachers and enough space give two more INUS conditions, as in figure II.2.

So this policy decision fell into the first of the two traps. It did not think enough about getting the support factors needed if the expected contribution were to be made. And their absence, or their inadequacy, will have eliminated or reduced the contribution of small class sizes to improved reading scores.

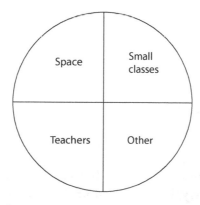

Figure II.2: A second cake for improved reading scores

It also fell into the other trap. It did not sufficiently take into account what other cakes, what other possible contributions, good or bad, might be relevant in the Californian situation, in particular how the introduction of the policy might affect those contributions. Small classes aren't the only thing that can contribute to better reading scores. We have already mentioned homework, but there are many others. Some of these can play positive causal roles; others, negative. In implementing policy, it is important to be careful not to introduce cakes that make negative contributions and not to eliminate good ones already in place.

This is one of the galling things that happened in California. The very process of implementing smaller classes there created a negative impact. When the class-size reduction program was implemented, there was not enough spare space to house the smaller classes. Space was found, but it was not as good as existing classrooms. That is what affected the contribution of the small class cake. Its support factors were not present. That is about the first trap.

But, in addition, and this is about the second trap, space was taken away from other activities that generally make positive contributions to good reading scores independently of class size—special needs, music and arts, athletics, and child care programs. One other cake that affects reading scores is the cake that has to do with the contribution of special needs teaching. That policy requires support factors if it is to make a contribution. Among them are good classrooms. But the class-size policy took that support away by requiring extra space. So that cake, the special needs cake, pictured in figure II.3, stopped making its positive contribution to the overall reading score effect, or its contribution was reduced.

Look at the cake in figure II.4, which like figures II.1, II.2, and II.3 produces a contribution to reading scores, but with a different policy variable again, and (some) different members of the support team. This cake is a member of the same family as are those in figures II.1, II.2, and II.3 because it makes a contribution to the same effect.

Here, higher reading scores are achieved by the presence of all of:

- Tutorial space
- Tutor's ability
- Student motivation
- Adequate hours of tutorials
- Student ability
- Other

We have stressed that if you want to bet on what the overall outcome will be, you will need a very thorough horizontal search, since you will need to consider all the cakes that will make a significant contribution. But even if

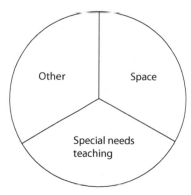

Figure II.3: A third cake for improved reading scores

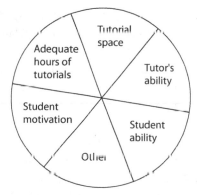

Figure II.4: A fourth cake for improved reading scores

you wish only to predict whether you will get an improvement over what would otherwise happen, it is still worthwhile to consider other cakes. First, because they can suggest other policies to you that might be effective enough yet be less costly or more acceptable, since generally no particular cake is necessary. There is more than one cake that can contribute to better test scores. We have introduced both class size reduction and homework to make this vivid. Second, to ensure you think about whether the process of implementing the policy as it probably will be done will add negative contributions or will remove factors that would otherwise have made positive contributions for you.

II.A.5 MORE EXAMPLES OF CAKES

Here is another example. Should you mandate using bicycle helmets to reduce head injuries?[2] Common sense, which is based on such things as observation of how things work, for instance, that protected heads get

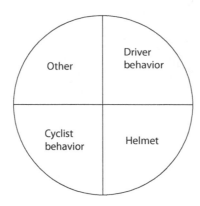

Figure II.5: A cake for reduction in head injuries to cyclists

injured less than unprotected ones, says yes. But why, then, do time-series studies in many jurisdictions that have passed helmet laws show no decrease in head injuries, or even increases?

The cake approach may help to order your thinking about this. Certainly wearing a helmet is a good candidate for being a factor in reducing head in-juries in cyclists. The common sense reasons based on repeated, if unsystem-atic, observational evidence, and on what is known about heads, are good reasons. But, thinking about it, you realize that the behavior of other drivers matters. They may give less space to cyclists with helmets because there is less chance of hurting them. And cyclists may take more risks because of a false sense of security. So the cake looks like the one in figure II.5.

This neatly illustrates two of our central points about the cake idea. First, it makes you think about what else has to be present, what support factors, if you are going to get the result you want. Second, a factor can be an ingre-dient in a good cake—wearing helmets will work if cyclists are trained not to become more reckless and drivers do not become less cautious, or an ingredient in a bad cake—more people get killed from wearing helmets on roads where car drivers become a great deal more thoughtless as a result, or cyclists more reckless.

II.A.6 SOME COMPLICATIONS

First, in our discussion of homework and class size, we have been concerned only with the reading score effect. So special needs teaching from figure II.3 only gets into the discussion because it may contribute to that. But plainly the policy as implemented could reduce the contribution of special needs teaching not only to reading scores but to the education of special needs children more generally. That is another important aspect of a policy decision. It may affect not only the target variable, the desired outcome, but also other outcomes that matter to you, but that you are not focusing on.

So the notion of unintended consequences covers at least two possibilities. One is that implementing your policy may indeed make a good contribution to what you are aiming to achieve in the ways you have thought about, as part of one cake. But it may bring about a bad contribution in ways you have not thought about because it affects another cake. Another is that it may bring about a bad contribution to something quite different that you are not thinking about.

Second complication—you usually can't hope to know what all the cakes are, both positive and negative, that have your policy as an ingredient, and what all the support factors are, even if you make heroic efforts at listing cakes and their support factors. So even well-warranted policies will often unexpectedly fail. We can't fix that, nor can you. But a thoughtful horizontal search can help you do better. Our analysis is designed to reduce error in deciding policy by eliminating illegitimate short cuts. It cannot provide any guarantee that, without short cuts, you will always make reliable predictions.

Third, because we started by asking whether a policy of promoting homework would increase test scores, the "homework" ingredient of the cake may be privileged in your thinking because it is the policy variable the social engineer hopes to manipulate to achieve the desired contribution. So the other factors in the cake are called "the support factors," to fit with the typical starting point for a policy debate "Should we do this to get that?" thereby foregrounding "this." This practice is harmless, provided that you recognize that the support factors are just as important in this cake as is the policy—if any one of the ingredients is absent, you will not achieve the contribution.

This is a particular example of a general problem—why it is that certain factors in the cake come to be salient in our thinking. We have a section on this below in II.A.7. Salience matters because it often brings with it its converse—the neglect of other factors that on our account, and as a matter of fact, in many policy contexts are as important as the salient factor. Because small classes seemed such an obviously good idea for California, it was natural not to focus on the tiresome details of teacher and classroom availability. This tendency is closely linked to the problem of our appetite for silver bullets, trumps, and magical thinking generally. On this, too, we have something to say, also in II.A.7.

Fourth, a factor that is favorable in one cake may be unfavorable in another. An isolated study space at home may be just what is needed to enable a well-motivated child to do her homework. It may also be just what is needed to enable a badly motivated child to spend time texting her friends as she could not if she were working in the living room under the eyes of her family. So good study space can make things worse.

Fifth, it may be that every one of the ingredients is necessary, but that another factor, not in the cake, may be a good substitute for the factor that is. That is one way of generating another cake that contributes to the same effect. Absence of parental support can be made up for by favorable peer pressure—being at a school where academic success really matters. This is plainly a factor in elite British schools.

Sixth, the same factor, for example, teacher quality, may appear in many cakes. As we say below, in II.A.7, this is one (good) reason why a particular factor may become salient, and (rightly) trump other factors.

Seventh, as we have repeatedly urged, it will be difficult to predict what actual value of reading scores to expect. But it can even be difficult to predict in what direction your policy will act compared to what would have happened otherwise. That's because, as we warned, you may in the very act of implementing policy introduce factors that play a negative role or remove ones that play a positive role without realizing it.

Eighth, the cake model is about necessary conditions. If you don't have enough teachers, you don't get the result. This is an extreme binary outcome. The policy is there or not; the effect obtains or not. But often you can have more or less of a policy and may expect more or less of the effect. With a smaller quantity of one of the ingredients you get less of a contribution; with larger quantities for the ingredients, larger contributions. Better teachers contribute to better reading scores. The basic lesson though is still the same. To get the size of a contribution you expect, all the necessary ingredients for it must be there together and they must all take on the right values to produce a contribution of the desired size. If you are willing to settle for a smaller contribution, then maybe you can do with a different cake, say one with the same ingredients but just smaller quantities of some of them. In any case, the policy is only one ingredient and you will need all the other ingredients to be there as well—and be of the right magnitude—to get the contribution of the size you want.

Ninth, if, as you will, you have a number of cakes that can, or do, make a contribution, good or bad, we have assumed that the cakes combine to produce the total effect by addition. This will not always be the case. You already know this from elementary physics where simple addition is not the rule; rather, forces combine by vector addition. Threshold effects are also commonplace: contributions add till you hit a ceiling; then adding more cakes won't make any difference. These are complications that can matter to your case and that you need to keep an eye out for. But before that, you must worry about what ingredients you need for a complete cake if your policy is to make a contribution at all, and what other bad cakes might be around undoing its good effects. After that there is no end to the variety of possible complications. We use simple standard assumptions to drive home our central points and to make our account manageable. But that does not mean that life is so simple.

Tenth, cakes cannot represent the dynamics of the causal process that is meant to start with the policy and end with the desired effect. But, as we discuss in III.B.2, understanding just what that process is can often be of great help since unanticipated breakdowns somewhere in the middle are altogether too common. The causal process proceeds step-by-step, each step producing the one following. Each step in the process is, as is usual with causation, only an INUS condition for the next step. Step 2 is only one of a number of ingredients in the cake that will produce step 3, and step 3 is only one of a number of ingredients necessary for step 4, and so forth. That is, each step has its own necessary support factors. If the policy at the start is to produce the desired effect at the end, all the support factors from all the cakes have to be in place at the right times.

So when we talk of the INUS conditions—the ingredients in the cake—that are necessary for the policy to produce the final effect, we are talking about the whole set of all these support factors, gathered into one. Unfortunately, the cake image does not make the time sequence conspicuous. It is important to keep this in mind because time variation in support factors matters. Each ingredient in the cake must be in place at the right time or the effect will be threatened. It is not enough to have enough teachers in place at the beginning of the school year if they all leave for better paid jobs at Christmas. Better methods for representing the process step-by-step are described in Appendix I, but these are, of necessity, more complicated and demanding. We stick with the cakes notation because it provides a simple graphic image of what you need.

Eleventh, you may be accused of failure even if your policy makes a significant positive contribution. Sometimes things are on a downhill trend—they are getting worse independently of your policy and its implementation. In that case your policy can be very successful. It can make a big positive contribution so that matters are far better than they otherwise would have been. But they are still worse after the policy than before. And your policy will—mistakenly—be judged a failure.

This is one of the motives for introducing policies in a way that allows for good post hoc evaluation that can provide a comparison of those who were subject to the policy and individuals in just the same circumstances in the targeted setting who were not. But, of course, such studies are exceedingly difficult to do. Moreover, some polices that might be very effective will not readily lend themselves to study designs that can do this reliably, and the demand that they be evaluable in this way can distort policy.

Britain's Sure Start program may be an example here. At the core of the program was the idea that different communities have different factors already in place to help children be healthier and get a better start at school, so that decisions about what concrete changes to put in place should be decided according to the special needs of each community. But, critics who wanted gold standard evidence about whether the policy worked or not complained that this made the "treatment" too heterogeneous to afford a good RCT-design evaluation.

Twelfth, and so on.

The cake metaphor gives plenty of opportunity for sprawling taxonomy. There is only so much that it can do. It is not here to provide an exhaustive and systematic guide to thinking of everything. What it does is to suggest an approach. When presented with a policy proposal—that this intervention will produce the desired result here—we suggest that you set about constructing cakes, good and bad, and searching out the requisite ingredients in them. If this is done as best you can, and you have set up a family of cakes, linked by commonality of outcomes, you will have made the right start to answering questions such as:

- What support factors have to be present if my policy variable is to produce the contribution I want?
- Are there many ways that my policy might make a good contribution? Is it a member of many good cakes?
- Are there many ways in which my policy might make a bad contribution? Is it a member of many bad cakes?
- If the support factors are not all there, what happens? Nothing? Or less? Or something bad? Does the absence of a support factor turn a good cake into a bad cake? Or vice versa?
- Are there other ways, other policies, that produce the same result? What about their cake families?

II.A.7 SALIENCE, TRUMPS, AND NO BRAINERS

Talking about support factors, we were careful to emphasize that strictly there is no hierarchy among ingredients in a cake—each ingredient represents a necessary condition, and the cake as a whole is sufficient to contribute to the effect. We made this good by saying that *all* the ingredients in figures II.1 through II.5 have to be present. But we all share a very strong instinct that some ingredients, some factors, matter more than others. Surely it is right or at least harmless to say that it is the aspirin that cures the headache. And that indeed may be harmless, so long as you know what you are doing, and that you see the aspirin as no more than salient in the analysis—sticking out for some reason.

The reasons include the following:

1. If a factor appears in many more cakes than does any other, or indeed in all cakes, it remains true that in any particular cake it is unprivileged. But it is certainly privileged by ubiquity and hence salient for anyone wanting to know how to achieve the effect. This is the case that backs our account of the quick exit decision tree strategy in III.B.4.
2. If it never seems to do any harm. It is never a member of a bad cake.
3. If it is what was added yesterday and the world changed today. It may be that every ingredient of the good cake is necessary. But if every one of them was present yesterday except ingredient X, ingredient X will get the credit, just as it is the last straw that breaks the camel's back.
4. If you discover by chance that vaccination with cowpox goes with immunity to small pox, or even more, if that is so of a novel herb recently imported from Sumatra, that will make the herb salient.
5. A factor will be salient if a politician makes it so. If the new government wants to believe that withdrawing benifits will drive people back to work, and careful analysis shows that there is indeed a good causal cake to back that, and the policy does indeed work, it is natural to make that ingredient of the cake salient.
6. If a policy requires few support factors, or if it is "obvious," a "no brainer" that all the support factors are there, it is natural to treat the policy variable as a trump, as for practical purposes the only member of the cake, as both necessary and sufficient, and therefore unambiguously The Cause of the effect. So if you want to terrorize the enemy into submission, drop a nuclear bomb. Even in this case, you need to give *some* consideration to, for example, the morale of the enemy and their capability to persevere in the face of appalling losses.
7. All decision making requires short cuts. Just as some factors are salient, some are the opposite—they are background, not worth spending time on. There are better things to do when considering policy than to proliferate support factors. It is true that if the sun does not rise tomorrow, assigning homework will not help reading scores. And maybe it won't because the Aztecs have failed to make the appropriate human sacrifices. But we are prepared to assume that the sun rising is not a relevant support factor that needs to be put in the cake. If the relevance and presence of *all* the support factors are no brainers, then we have a trump.
8. It is natural to err on the side of identifying, or hoping for, trumps— what are sometimes called "magic bullets." They are very nice to have— they mean you don't have to think and that you are bound to succeed. Much of the impetus for evidence-based policy came from a concern that this temptation is very powerful for politicians, the public, and the media, and that, if it is indeed a limiting case, the magic bullet will be

rare, and that if we are to err, it should be in the other direction, of excessive concern to understand how things work rather than optimism that it is all very simple really.

II.A.8 CONCLUSION

In this part, we have deliberately avoided some of the complexities of the theory in I.B. We have attempted to aid understanding by taking simple examples, simple above all because they are typically limited to single cakes. Our account of how you deal with a multiplicity of cakes, good cakes, bad cakes, alternative cakes, how you combine good contributions with bad, has been cursory. That has been in the interests of enabling you to get a grasp of the elements of our approach.

But in II.A.2, with the example of Better Reading Scores, we give an example of how you have to go beyond your first cake before you decide to bet on your policy. The first cake in figure II.2 tells you that you need the right teachers and the right space. Figure II.3 tells you that you may, if you introduce smaller classes, disturb another good cake in which your policy does not figure, the cake that shows that special needs teaching needs those support factors too, and you are taking them away. Since special needs teaching is good for reading scores too, that means that the effect of your policy may not be as good as the first cake leads you to hope. It may even be negative. And then figure II.4 shows that there are other policies that make for better reading scores, like more homework.

Proliferating cakes like this is hard, as is populating them. It is a fertile source of error to assume that the search can be abbreviated by lighting on one bit of evidence—say, an RCT—that cuts through all the detail. Our cakes metaphor, and its parent, the theory with its talk of causal roles and support factors, give you a structure within which to look for what evidence you need, what facts fit into the argument that leads to an effectiveness conclusion. To that extent, it tells you all you need to in order to do. You just go on and on doing what the reading scores example shows. What it cannot guarantee is that your search will lead to a conclusive answer. At the end, you have to step back and decide whether your policy looks like a good bet. If you are lucky, very lucky, you may be able to predict actual outcomes. Perhaps the problem is simple, and there are just not very many cakes to think about. Perhaps, alas, all you end up with is that you do not understand very much about what the effect of your policy will be. But we will have helped you to make better predictions about whether introducing your policy will improve the targeted effect over what it otherwise would be.

The search will be hard and laborious. But it is also ordinary. It is what we do all the time, when we face decisions in business or personal life, legal or policy issues, which may seem banal, but share a common structure—that you had best think in terms of our approach. And there is no short cut.

CHAPTER II.B

⌒∿⌒

Causal Roles

Shared and Unshared

II.B.1 WHERE WE ARE AND WHERE WE ARE GOING

This chapter is about causal roles and especially about finding the right causal roles, ones that will travel from there to here, in order to make failures like those of the Bangladesh Integrated Nutrition Program less likely. Before turning to the basic ideas and then to Bangladesh, we will make a side trip through a less serious example that illustrates our point. Here is a story Nancy tells about her role in editing this book.

I like to edit on paper, and with a pencil, a sharp pencil. I sharpen my pencils by putting a kite outside my study window. Of course I know, as we rehearsed in II.A, that what I think of as "the cause" is likely to be only one ingredient in a causal cake. In my case I have to wait for a windy day or write with a pen. How is it that I can sharpen my pencils by flying a kite? I can do so because my study was designed by Rube Goldberg. It looks like figure II.6.

This is a very effective strategy for me. Indeed, the only one that works, since I don't have any other pencil sharpeners at my home and all my knives are dull. If you don't believe me, come and test it. Decide randomly, each day, whether the kite goes out the window or not. You will definitely get more sharp pencils in your treatment group than in your control group. And when I put the policy into practice I follow our advice from II.A about trying to maximize the good values for the support variables: I only put the kite out the window when I have good reason to think the wind will blow. So I am almost always successful.

Pencil Sharpener

The Professor gets his think-tank working and evolves the simplified pencil sharpener.

Open window (**A**) and fly kite (**B**). String (**C**) lifts small door (**D**), allowing moths (**E**) to escape and eat red flannel shirt (**F**). As weight of shirt becomes less, shoe (**G**) steps on switch (**H**) which heats electric iron (**I**) and burns hole in pants (**J**).

Smoke (**K**) enters hole in tree (**L**), smoking out opossum (**M**) which jumps into basket (**N**), pulling rope (**O**) and lifting cage (**P**), allowing woodpecker (**Q**) to chew wood from pencil (**R**), exposing lead. Emergency knife (**S**) is always handy in case opossum or the woodpecker gets sick and can't work.

Figure II.6: The pencil sharpener that works in Nancy's study. Reproduced with permission of Rube Goldberg Inc.

Still, I would not advise you to fly a kite to sharpen your pencils. Kite flying undoubtedly plays a causal role in the causal principle that governs pencil sharpening there in my study. But that principle is very local. The causal role played by kite flying will not travel. Because of that it doesn't matter how secure the experimental results are; they are irrelevant for predicting what will happen in your study.

That's the bad news. But there is good news. There are more stable, what we might call "more fundamental," roles to be found in my pencil sharpening process. And the success of the process in your experiment provides evidence for each of them. Of course, it is only evidence about those causal roles there, in my study. But for these principles we have a great deal—and importantly a great variety—of independent evidence that the causal roles are played more widely. Here are just a few, from the start of the machine:

1. Pulling on one end of a pulley rope can play a positive causal role in lifting weights at the other end.
2. Breaching a closed container can play a positive causal role in allowing the contents to escape.

3. Moths can play a positive causal role in getting rid of flannel.
4. Reducing the pull on one end of a pulley rope can play a positive causal role in lowering objects on the other end.

These facts about causal roles are worth knowing. They might help you build yourself a pencil sharpener that works even though it looks nothing like mine. This is what this chapter is about.

The bad news: beware, many well-evidenced causal roles do not travel. And the good news: but sometimes even the very same experiments that established those causal roles, there in the study setting, also provide evidence for other, less visible causal roles that will travel.

Before we begin to explain this in earnest, here's a reminder about terminology. Recall that causes are INUS conditions. Your policy will probably need support factors to make a contribution at all, and there will generally be other causal cakes that also make contributions, positive and negative. *Causal roles* are about each of these cakes separately. The policy *can play a causal role* in a given situation if it is part of a causal cake that is enough to make its own contribution to the effect in that situation. It *plays the same causal role* in one situation as in another if it is part of some cake in each place that produces a contribution of the same direction in both situations, regardless of what other causal cakes might contribute to that effect in the two situations or what the other ingredients in the contributing cake are in the two places. We will not generally be focusing here on the whole array of causal cakes that contribute but only on those that might contain the policy.

Note that we have talked here about what the cause *can* do—which means what it can contribute—rather than what it does contribute or what will actually result. For example, the cereal box: "Eating Golden Flakes can improve heart health." The *can* signifies that it is only one ingredient in a cake—it needs support factors—and that it is not the only thing that can contribute. If you don't exercise and you eat fish and chips five evenings a week you will probably not have very good heart health even if you do eat Golden Flakes every morning.

We shall also talk here about causal principles. The term *causal principle* is used in different ways. Two distinct uses matter here. First is the one we introduced in I.B. A causal principle for a situation expresses all the causal cakes responsible for the effect in that situation, what's in each cake, and how the contributions from the cakes combine. These fix just what will happen in the situation given the actual values of all the ingredients in all the cakes. In the other usage, a causal principle only lays out the contribution of a single cake. It is hard to avoid this second usage in talking about causal roles, which is our focus in this chapter. Every other way of talking becomes awkward. So we too shall employ this second use. But please don't get confused. What get called "causal principles" in this chapter fix only contributions, not the entire effect.

II.B.2 WHAT'S A VERTICAL SEARCH AND WHY IS IT ESSENTIAL?

Yesterday I used a hammer claw to pull a nail from the wall. You could say, and it would be right, that the result depended on the truth of the causal principle, "Hammer claws extract nails," even if few would think like that. The day before, I sat way at the end of a seesaw to lift three children into the air. You could say, and it would be right, that the result depended on the truth of the causal principle, "Sitting on the end of a seesaw raises children into the air at the other end," even if few would think like that.

What hammers and seesaws can do is part of our shared, commonsense knowledge about causes and what they can do. It is low level and specific, which is why we don't feel the need to express what they can do in terms of causal principles. A great deal of life is led, and successfully led, at this level.

At this low level the two causal principles are unrelated. They are separate principles about hammers, and about seesaws. Seesaws do not raise children because of what hammers can do, nor vice versa. But at another level, they are related. They are subsumed under a more abstract generalization a shared causal principle. Both depend on the more abstract principle of the lever: "A lever with a weight on one end can raise heavier objects at the other end, according to the formula $F_1D_1 = F_2D_2$," where the F's denote the forces at the ends and the D's, the distances from the fulcrum. This part of our book is about the importance of knowing what level you are at when you are relying on a causal principle.

There is always more than one correct way to describe what caused a result or justifies a prediction. Some of these ways will generalize across a great many cases, others across very few. In large part, getting that right depends on finding concepts at the right level of abstraction, or generality. The behavior of the hammer can be highly relevant for predicting the behavior of the seesaw—but only if you know you can correctly describe both as levers and you know how to describe the outcomes in both cases in terms of forces and distances, then retranslate to the effect on the nail and on lifting the children. To make the right prediction you first move up the ladder of abstraction, from "hammer claw" to "lever," to deploy a more general causal principle at a higher level of abstraction. Then to predict on the playground, you must move down the ladder of abstraction, from lever to "seesaw." Looking for the right steps to take up and down the ladder of abstraction is what we call *vertical search*.

II.B.3 FITTING LOCAL DESCRIPTIONS UNDER MORE ABSTRACT ONES

As with the hammer claw and lever, one and the same feature can instantiate causes at two different levels of abstraction at once, one more concrete and local, the other more abstract and general. That's why different principles involving factors at different levels of abstraction can all obtain at once. "You can raise a child with a seesaw" is true. "You can raise a child with a lever" is equally true because a seesaw is a lever. "The trajectories of bodies moving on a sphere subject only to inertia are great circles" is true; so too is "The trajectories of bodies moving on a sphere subject only to inertia are geodesics (i.e., the shortest distance between two points)." They are equally true because, on a sphere, a great circle *is* the shortest distance between two points, as you can see in figure II.7. The higher the level of abstraction of a causal principle, in general the more widely it is shared across situations. Remarks about hammers/nails, seesaws/children do not read across one to the other. But remarks about levers refer to both of them, and to many others.

Climbing up the vertical ladder is not just a matter of ex post classification or theorizing. Finding a term like "lever" that successfully groups separate phenomena, such as the behavior of hammers and seesaws, is also part of thinking about how to solve problems ex ante. For example, there is a big stone in the way. You have to move it six feet to the left. It is too heavy to roll. Most people know without having to think much that, if you get a crowbar, you can slowly but surely shift it. You probably recognize that without thinking about levers. But if you don't know about crowbars, you may say to yourself, "Isn't this something like my problem last week, when I couldn't get the nail out with pliers, and I had to use a hammer?" And you get the idea that this is something a lever might help with. And you end up with a crowbar.

That is a *vertical search*.

Then when asked you can say that you used a crowbar, or what is in this case the same thing, a lever. If you had been concerned to scare a burglar, you might also have said that you used a crowbar, or a weapon. But it would have been crazy to say that you used a lever. For example, a seesaw?

II.B.4 MALNUTRITION: A CASE STUDY

II.B.4.1 Bangladesh Integrated Nutrition Project (BINP)

One of the objectives of BINP was to improve the nutritional status of pregnant and lactating women, and of their infant children, in poor communities. The design drew heavily on the Tamil Nadu Integrated Nutrition

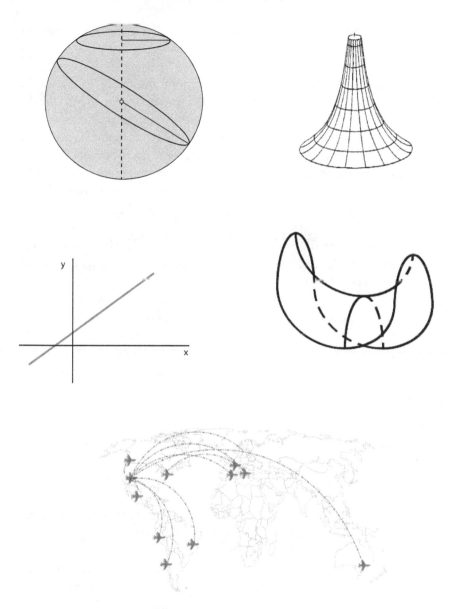

Figure II.7: What is a straight line?

Project (TINP), which had been deemed successful. BINP was to provide nutritional counseling for pregnant women, and supplementary feeding for children under 24 months who were especially deprived. Nutritional counseling was expected to be effective not only to make it more likely that the supplemental feeding improved nutrition for the children but also particularly to counteract poor nutrition of pregnant women and low birth weight babies arising from ignorance, for instance, from a belief in "eating down" during pregnancy to ease delivery by having smaller babies, and avoiding meat, fish, and eggs during pregnancy, thereby damaging the nutritional standards of both mother and child.

An analysis by the World Bank's Operations Evaluation Department found no significant impact on nutritional standards from BINP (World Bank 1995). This is despite the fact that this kind of program had "worked" in Tamil Nadu. What went wrong? The reasons for the lack of impact in Bangladesh, it seems, is that in Bangladesh there was food "leakage" and "substitution." The food was often not used as a supplement but as a substitute, with the supplementary food allowing the usual home food allocation for the mother and the children to leak to another member of the family.

Both these factors arose in part from what has been labeled "the mother-in-law factor" by Howard White, who also points out what might be called "the male-shopper factor":

> The program targeted the mothers of young children. But mothers are frequently not the decision makers, and rarely the sole decision makers, with respect to the health and nutrition of their children. For a start, women do not go to market in rural Bangladesh; it is men who do the shopping. And for women in joint households—meaning they live with their mother-in-law—as a sizeable minority do, then the mother-in-law heads the women's domain. (White 2009: 6)

So the improvement in nutritional knowledge for the pregnant mother about herself and her young children does not help if it is not she who controls what happens to the food, what food is available in the family, and how it is distributed.

Certainly, with hindsight, it is easy to fit these failures into the cake structure and say that the horizontal search succeeded in identifying two ingredients in the cake—"supply of supplementary food" and "nutritional counseling"—neither of which would work on its own. But it failed to identify the ingredient "the mother must have control." So maybe we just say that sometimes horizontal searches are hard or inadequate. We just didn't spot that there was another support factor, "mother's control," because it was present in Tamil Nadu and so was never salient. And it only became salient in Bangladesh when its absence mattered.

You could say that, and it would be correct, and it would mesh nicely with what we have preached, that you should have a serious concern to identify what support factors are necessary and to secure them. But we want to suggest a different way to look at it, a way that allows scientific results to help you build new policy programs different from those that have already been tried, with a good chance of success. As it stands, the

Tamil Nadu study is irrelevant to the villages where Bangladesh wants to work to improve child nutrition. The principle that "mother's control + mother's nutritional counseling + supply of supplementary food can improve nutrition in the children" would do to explain the failure in Bangladesh, where the mother does not have control. But it is no help in working out what *would* work in Bangladesh.

But the idea of vertical search, of a hierarchy of abstraction, helps you to see why the horizontal search failed, and how you might better spot support factors other than too late when they become salient by their absence.

Why did it turn out that the results in Tamil Nadu were not evidentially relevant to predictions about the success of the policy in Bangladesh? They should have been. Just as you can characterize the effect of the hammer in removing the nail under the principle that hammers can remove nails (a principle you can recognize without any higher level thoughts, for example, about levers), so in this case it is natural to start by characterizing the choice of knowledge plus feeding as the operation of the low-level principle:

> Principle 1: Better nutritional knowledge in mothers plus supply of supplementary food can improve the nutritional status of their infants.

This is a principle based on observation of success elsewhere, without higher level thoughts.

But in fact the two populations did not share this principle. This principle was true in the original successful cases but not in Bangladesh. To get a shared principle that covers both, it seems that what's needed instead is:

> Principle 2: Better nutritional knowledge in mothers plus *supplemental feeding of their infants* can improve the infants' nutrition.

This is a principle that uses concepts at a *higher level of abstraction*. In the successful cases in India, the more concrete feature "food supplied by the project" constituted the more abstract feature "supplemental feeding," but it did not do so in Bangladesh. Not getting this straight is a failure of *vertical search*: a failure to identify the right level of abstraction to find common explanatory elements.

Still, Principle 2 is not shared between Tamil Nadu sites and those in Bangladesh either, because of the mother-in-law and male-shopper problems. Recognizing this suggests yet another vertical move to secure a shared principle:

> Principle 3. Better nutritional knowledge can improve infants' nutrition if the persons who have the knowledge are those who

a. provide the child with supplemental food

b. control what food is procured

c. control how food gets dispensed

d. hold the child's interests as central in performing a, b, and c.

Just as the supply of supplementary food did not count as supplemental feeding of the infant in the Bangladesh program, because somebody else ate the supplemental food supplied, mothers in that program did not in general satisfy the more abstract descriptions in a, b, and c.

So we have climbed up the vertical ladder of abstraction from Principal 1 to Principle 3, gaining generality as we go. But we have to climb down again to see how Principle 3 is translated into facts on the ground in Bangladesh. How does this relate to horizontal search and support factors?

First, you could construct three good cakes, with support factors and policy variables, one for each of the three levels or principles.

Second, all the ingredients for each of the three cakes obtained in Tamil Nadu. And in Tamil Nadu all three cakes, at all three levels of abstraction, were sufficient for a positive outcome. The *ingredients* for cakes 1 and 2 obtained in Bangladesh sites as well. But that didn't help in Bangladesh. Unlike Tamil Nadu, these factors do not play a causal role in Bangladesh. In Bangladesh only the highest level cake is sufficient to produce a contribution to the outcome, and the ingredients for that cake just weren't there in Bangladesh.

Third, the higher the level of abstraction at which the cake sits, the more likely it is that its ingredients, if all are present, are sufficient to improve outcomes. That's a help in reasoning about whether a tested policy will work for you, but only a partial help. You still have to figure out how to get back down the ladder of abstraction, to figure out what those ingredients amount to on the ground, in your case, if you are to get what you want.

II.B.4.2 Specifics and Generalizations

To illustrate more about the structure of vertical search, take an extended version of the story about nutritional education and supplemental feeding. This story is based on the Tamil Nadu case; but it is hypothetical, and that allows us to be a little less impersonal and more wide-ranging than can the World Bank's report. It can be more low-level and about a very particular case. That helps to reinforce the important lesson that successful policies work if and only if they work at the lowest level of generality, at the level of the absolutely specific.

You can start the analysis with an even lower principle than Principle 1—indeed, so specific a statement that it looks like a limiting case, a principle that has lost all the generality required to make it a principle.[1]

> Principle A. If Fatima learns not to eat down during pregnancy, and she is provided with maize, her and her baby's and Abdul and Leyla's nutrition can improve, if Ayesha does not interfere

where Fatima is the mother, Abdul and Leyla the children, Ayesha the mother-in-law. This is the effective cake, the one that delivers the result for Fatima, her baby, and Abdul and Leyla.

So far, even if you have a successful experience with Fatima, Abdul, and Leyla, you cannot apply Principle A to another family, let alone another country because proper names are not descriptions. This is the rock bottom case of a specific experience that cannot be generalized even to another similar family, let alone another country. Principle A is equivalent *in this case* to:

> Principle B. If the mother learns not to eat down, and she is provided with maize during pregnancy, her, and her baby's, and the children's nutrition can improve, if the mother-in-law does not interfere.

But Principle B may well not apply in a (fictitious) African village. There, the food is wheat. After a certain age, the eldest female child hands out the food to everyone including the mother, because the mother works. And it is the father who may interfere, because he sells the wheat on the market to buy tools. And nobody eats enough during Ramadan. And damaging beliefs about eating during pregnancy do not apply. This suggests:

> Principle AA. If you teach Suhaila how to feed the children enough during Ramadan, she will give wheat to Komnan and Ameyo, and their nutrition can improve, provided Sulaiman does not sell the wheat for tools.

where Suhaila is the eldest daughter, Sulaiman the father, and Komnan and Ameyo the children. Principle AA is equivalent *in this case* to:

> Principle BA. If you teach the elder sister how to feed the children enough during Ramadan, and you give her food, children's nutrition can improve, provided the father does not sell the food for tools.

This principle is quite different from the similar Bangladeshi Principle B.

So to link the Bangladesh and the experience from this African village, you have to go back to the original Principle 3, here Principle C:

> Principle C. Better nutritional knowledge can result in better children's nutrition in those who
> a. provide the child with supplemental feeding
> b. control what food is procured
> c. control how food gets dispensed
> d. hold the child's interests as central in performing a, b, and c.

We can, of course, go higher and higher up the ladder of abstraction, up to the top:

> Principle Z. To solve any problem, give the right resources to the right agents in the right circumstances.

This is (nearly) vacuous. It illustrates the important point that the higher the level of the principle, the harder it is to climb down from it to the level B principle that is the only one that has any actual effect. High level principles have the virtue that they apply to large numbers of cases—there are very many lower level principles that exemplify them. But identifying what these lower level principles are is very hard. Just think how you would make Principle Z translate into Principle BA in Africa.

Science gives you principles at a level higher than B, or a fortiori than A. The formula about levers, "A lever with a weight on one end can raise heavier objects at the other end, according to the formula $F_1 D_1 = F_2 D_2$," does not tell you to use a hammer or a seesaw here. There is always a danger that, as you climb higher and higher, the principles become more and more general and harder and harder to translate into lower level operational principles.

The lever formula is a long way from being vacuous or nonoperational. But the economic notion of Utility looks dangerously general in the hands of, for example, Gary Becker. Becker won the Nobel Prize for modeling great swathes of what we do in day-to-day life under the principles of market equilibrium and rational choice theory, from drug addiction to racial discrimination to crime and family relations. Becker supposes that the agents he models act so as to maximize their expected utility. At that level of generality, say Principle U, we people are really much the same at base, governed by the same motivations and the same principles of human nature. The difficulty, or the trick, is to determine just what, in the case under study, utility consists in, which can include anything from financial gains to inconvenience to serious illness or the joys of watching your spouse have a good time. What, in fact, are the principles like B and A that operate here? What does "utility" mean here? This enterprise is relatively unconstrained, so that too much can count as utility. If (almost) anything goes, the principle gives very little help in the here and now.

II.B.4.3 A Caricature Genealogy

You send out to Bangladesh an aid worker who is intelligent and profession-ally serious but has no training in nutrition or anything that might help with the problem that stares her in the face in all the villages in her territory—child malnutrition. She has, of course, common sense, meaning a heteroge-neous collection of background knowledge and beliefs from her experience of life so far.

So she sets to work. Common sense tells her, "Give them food," which means to her porridge, of which she can lay her hands on more than enough for her to experiment in the village that she has chosen for her pilot. So she gives Fatima porridge for Abdul and Leyla.

And she slowly but surely (she is intelligent) goes through the steps set out in the examples. She realizes that oats won't do; it has to be maize, and that Fatima won't use the extra food in the right way because of her belief in eating down. And anyway Ayesha won't let her. By various stratagems she succeeds in improving the nutrition of Abdul and Leyla.

So far, she has not had to think in terms of principles, of generalizations, at all. She is dealing with one family throughout, with oats and maize, with Fatima, Ayesha, Abdul, and Leyla. She does not have to think about them under other descriptions—mother, child, mother-in-law, food. She has solved the problem specifically without climbing higher.

But next she realizes that she could help other families in the region. And that policy requires generalizing. She has to produce a principle like Prin-ciple B. She has to talk about mothers, not about Fatima. And if then she proposes that the insights gained in Bangladesh be used in Africa, she has to produce a principle like Principle C.

But it is no help to produce something like Principle Z, true as it is. That is because, by the time that you have climbed up the ladder to Z, you have reached a principle that is so general that it gives you no purchase when you try to climb down again. "To solve any problem, give the right resources to the right agents in the right circumstances" gives you no help in clambering down to A or B or C. And clamber down is what you have to do. You have to say what (if any) is the valid principle B in Africa, and who are the people in that family who instantiate that principle to produce Principle A. The notion that you have to apply general principles correctly to particular cases if you are to adopt the right policies is unimpeachable. So, too, the notion that general principles are based on particular cases.

To ask whether this case is like that (whether it will work here because it worked there) is to ask whether the two cases are similar in the relevant respects. The lowest level description does not help with that. But the next principle up tells you what may be relevant respects—is the mother educated? Does the mother-in-law interfere? Even if the comparison passes that test, you still have to move up to Principle C. It may not be the mother-in-law who interferes. And the higher you get, the less helpful the process becomes. If you are comparing malnutrition in poor white communities in North Carolina with Bangladesh, you may have to go higher up the ladder. Not maybe to Z. But suppose you have to go up to

Principle F. Give the children the right food in the right circumstances.

Now this is not vacuous. But you have now arrived at no more than a very generic nutritional fact. And that gives you nothing much to work on if you are trying to find out what goes on in North Carolina. It makes the fact that TINP worked of no use. You have to get right down to Jane and Joe Doe to see what goes wrong when you give them food parcels. Like the aid worker, you have to start with the particular case to see what generalizations you can formulate. And there is no reason to think that if you find such generalizations, they will fall under your Principle C. And if they only fall under F or even Z, then the similarities between North Carolina, Bangladesh, and Africa have become vanishingly small.

Causal roles often don't travel. Factors that play a causal role for the outcome you want in one setting, perhaps producing a very substantial contribution indeed, may play no causal role at all in yours. This is especially likely if these factors are very concrete. It seems that factors that play the same causal role across a wide variety of situations may have to be factors at a fairly high level of abstraction. Like a lever.

PART THREE

Strategies for Finding What You Need to Know

CHAPTER III.A

✦

Where We Are and Where We Are Going

E ven if a policy has been proven to work elsewhere, perhaps even in a good many elsewheres, it won't work for you, we have urged, if you cannot secure the requisite support factors that are needed for it to operate, or if you have not climbed to the right level on the ladder of abstraction, to identify the description under which the policy works widely enough to reach your situation. Identifying the support factors is what we call "horizontal search"; identifying the right level of abstraction and figuring out what that amounts to for your situation—that is, identifying features that can genuinely play a positive causal role in your situation—is called "vertical search." In II.A and II.B, we left largely unexplored how you are meant to do that. Here in III we give some general strategies for engaging in these searches, for how to go about them.

In the ideal, you would not need these suggestions. A combination of the natural, social, and medical sciences, along with technology—engineering and social engineering—should have done the job for you. Like buying a car. Most of the support factors that cars need to work properly are built in, and others—gasoline, oil, water, brake fluid, and the like—are clearly indicated or well known; cars have been manufactured so that they can be expected to work across a wide range of situations; and reasonably accessible knowledge tells you which kinds of cars work better in which special circumstances: SAABs if you want them to start in bitter cold weather, Range Rovers for rough, muddy countryside.

That's hard to do for social policies. It would be nice if social policy were like a battery. Everything necessary for it to create a current is locked inside the casing; the environment it is to be put to work in is both structured and delimited, like a flashlight or a radio; and there are clear instructions for how it is to be implemented—"Put the end marked + here." But for social policies, the requisite scientific and technological knowledge and know-how is often missing. Scientists usually do RCTs to establish causal claims because they don't know what the necessary helping and hindering factors are for the policies under test. The environments under which you want your policies to work are open and unstructured, and social situations vary a great deal more, and in ways that matter, than do flashlights or radios.

Some of what you may read suggests exactly the opposite. Strict program fidelity is urged—do it just the way it was done in places where it worked. We discuss the pros and cons of this advice in IV.D. For now it suffices to stress that we are wary of this advice, since there is no warrant for assuming that the same policy will work here as there without well warranted answers to questions about causal roles and support factors.

This advice does have at least this advantage: you don't need to think much. Find an RCT that shows that the policy that you propose contributed to your desired effect there. Then introduce it here, and be careful to be faithful to the program specifications. Whatever its defects may be, this approach has one huge attraction—it is operational. It tells you what to do.

More important, it tells you what to do if you wish to delegate decisions to operatives on the ground. You cannot, and will not, at the center decide in each individual case, this day, here, what to do. But you can make sure that the operatives make that decision well by giving them a rule book. They must only make interventions that are supported by the evidence. This is what evidence-based policy is about. In V we look in greater detail at the implications for our approach of the insight that guides for conducting evidence-based policy are a delegation device, where the delegation is designed not to leave discretion to the operatives.

For us, one alternative would be to say that we, too, want to delegate decisions to the operatives, and we, too, do not want to leave them with any discretion. To make that good, we would have to write a rule book better than the other guides currently available. Such a rule book would have to set out how to get at the facts needed for effective interventions other than by just faithfully implementing something that has passed a good test, like an RCT, which we do not accept. And it might appear that in putting forward the notions of horizontal and vertical search, we are beginning to set out such a rule book—a set of procedures that leave little discretion to the operative.

But that is not the way we see it. We see horizontal and vertical searches as frameworks for organizing the facts needed for evidence-based policy, not as a set of rules. And it is apparent that our frameworks do not tell you enough for you to just do what they say without thinking much, as a good rule book or manual does. The process, for example, of climbing up and down the ladder of abstraction requires insight into both the question "Of what general causal role is this low-level program description an example?" and the question "Does our version of the program instantiate that role?" Neither is nailed down by our account of the searches so far, nor will they be here in III.

This is for a reason. Not only is the kind of information you need not nailed down by us in this book, but it cannot be. We do not believe that by further and more detailed explication of these ideas we can get to the point that you might like advice manuals to get to, where the operator can take up the rule book and, without exercising much or any discretion, do what is required. We do not think that it is possible to produce unambiguous rules for predicting the results of social policies. So, we do not think that we can produce these rules. So in our world, those who make the decisions will have to deliberate using their judgment and discretion.

Failing to find a rule book does not indicate incompetence but, rather, a principled difficulty that thinking is unavoidably open-ended. Here we want to underline merely that you—or someone on your behalf—will have to think, and think specifically about your situation. And you should not be afraid that this is second best. For most social problems, thinking is just what is necessary to get good predictions. Nor is this an unfamiliar exercise. It is what you do all the time, both in your own lives day-by-day, and in planning more generally and more widely. These are points we shall discuss further in V.

What we aim to do here in III is to suggest some strategies that will help you think—some devices that will help you do better at both horizontal and vertical searches. These are:

III.B.1: The Pre-mortem
III.B.2: Thinking Step-by-Step and Thinking Backwards
III.B.3: It Works. By Means of What?
III.B.4: Decisions Using Quick Exit Trees

CHAPTER III.B

⌒⊱⌒

Four Strategies

III.B.1 THE PRE-MORTEM

One very good way to come up with a list of factors that are necessary for your policy to work for you is to imagine that the policy hasn't worked.[1] Imagine that you have put the policy in place, just as you are planning to do it. And things have gone awry. You didn't get the outcomes you predicted. What went wrong? What could be the reasons that it didn't work?

This is a strategy that people employ all the time, possibly without realizing it. We shall illustrate with an example,[2] a decision that Jeremy was involved in. It is an example of predicting effectiveness in a business setting, not a social policy. We like that because it shows that our approach works for a wide variety of problems. There is nothing specialized about what we are proposing.

Videoconferencing has been around for some time now. It is a technically quite mature industry. There will be improvements, particularly in cost and speed. But the betting is that in 10 years' time what is on offer will differ from what we see today only because of incremental changes—more of the same, but better.

There is one exception to this. Many meetings—whether they are no more than between the high street banker and the mortgage client, or, at the other extreme, two rooms of lawyers and executives finalizing a deal between London and Tokyo—need to end with a legally binding real signature or signatures that both sides can see. There are fairly satisfactory ways of dealing with this, for example, electronic signatures. But if you want the real thing, it may not always be enough, as is often done, for me to sign at my end, and for my lawyers to say I have done so, and to send the original document to the other remote party later. At present, if I am in Tokyo and you are in London, we cannot both provide a wet signature to the same document in the same place at the same time. Nor can I sign a document in London that has to be in Tokyo in an hour.

In 2008, a Canadian company claimed to be well on the way to solving this problem. It said that it had a working prototype—called *LongPen*—that enables me to sign a document in London with a real pen linked via the internet to a robotically controlled pen in Tokyo, that writes a wet signature on the document in Tokyo, in ink, with the same pressure and in every respect identically as the London pen has written. That's the story.

How did Jeremy set about thinking about whether to invest in this business? First, he made a list of questions that needed to be answered:

1. Are such signatures legally binding?
2. Is the technology protected by patents?
3. How good/bad are the alternatives?
4. Will the pen work well enough in the real situations it is intended for?
5. Who are the actual and potential competitors?
6. Have the inventors enough money and management resources to make a go of it?
7. What are the needs this is meant to satisfy?
8. Do the people with those needs have any money?

The question this book helps answer is question 4. Will it work in the settings where it is supposed to? Will it work here? That question is what the causal cake metaphor helps you to think about. That is not to say that the other questions are less important—it is, for example, a commonplace in business that having an effective technology that works is not the same as having a product that sells. But, just as we said in I.A.5 about policy, we do not deal with all aspects—for example, it would be too expensive, or the politics wouldn't work. So, too, here in business, the cake technique does not deal with everything.

So turn to question 4. Jeremy goes into the Tech Garage, as it is called, and sees the demonstration. One of the technicians signs a document with the real pen and sure enough at the other end of the garage the robot pen produces an indistinguishable wet signature. But all this shows is that in this context this device succeeded, once. In our language, "it worked there." What did he need to know to predict that it will work here, for a customer who buys it and sets it up in her office? Everybody knows that prototypes don't always work in the field.

He needed to think about what complications there might be in practice. Because the device is needed for transactions that are very important for the parties, and must be legally binding, absolute confidence that it will work in many specific contexts is critical. Any suspicion that the signature may not appear, or may be distorted, undercuts the legally and psychologically necessary belief that the device can do no wrong.

So he imagined a real situation: one group of lawyers and clients gathered in an office in Tokyo and another in London. The distant writing device has been set up ahead of time and the document is now fed into it. The signatory in London takes the pen in hand and writes her signature in the panel indicated. And it does not appear properly on the document in Tokyo. That's bad news. What went wrong? Here's a list of problems:

- If the signatory had not used it before, she may have been nervous and done a bad signature. Even though it was perfectly reproduced, nobody, including her, thought that it was her signature.
- The technician who demonstrated the prototype is used to signing on the slightly slippery pad used for the original signature. Maybe the signatory found it hard to sign well on that surface. Indeed, maybe most people would.
- Maybe the signatory pressed very hard, or wrote too fast, or used a ballpoint pen . . .
- Maybe she spilled coffee on it, which happens more often than we like to think.
- Maybe it wasn't plugged in.
- Or ran out of ink.
- Across the room is one thing; London to Tokyo is another. Maybe distance matters.
- Or temperature in the room.
- Maybe a standard Internet connection of the kind they were trying to use wasn't good enough.
- Perhaps the device had degenerated with use. Did it get out of alignment; maybe the key components are not robust? Maybe it is moody, difficult, and sensitive.
- A rubber band plays a surprisingly important part in regulating the movement of the robotic pen. That looks like an easy thing to have gone wrong.
- Maybe its workings are easy to disturb and it was thrown out of operation by too much bumping around while transporting it to the office and setting it up there.
- Computers freeze, have to be rebooted. Maybe this software system is like that.

The list translates directly into a set of support factors that may be necessary if the machine is to work properly, in the field, for the people who buy it. Of course, the fact that we imagine that something might be a support factor doesn't mean that it is. Some things are no-brainers. Clearly the machine must be plugged in if it is to work. But many take thought, inquiry, or investigation to decide whether they are necessary. Anything that seems a plausible worry, you need to find out about. And when you can't find out, as will be the case with many things on the list—and many things you didn't even think to put on the list—you should be more cautious in your prediction. To the extent that you aren't sure about what is, and what isn't, a necessary support factor, and which of these you have in your situation and which you don't, to that extent you had better rein in your confidence that it will work for you.

Thinking about causal cakes might, at first glance, seem daunting, overly technical, and difficult to do in real life. What this example suggests is that you think like this all the time, and that the process is banal, not super intelligent. When you want to know if an intervention, decision, product, or policy will be effective in implementation, a pre-mortem is a good way to get started.

In thinking about this Canadian product, Jeremy was doing just that. He wanted to know if, in actual rollout and use, the product would be effective in the specific kinds of situations it was likely to be used in. He asked the developers about some common problems that we're all familiar with in an office setting: spilled coffee, bad Internet connections, poor reliability of electronic tools, and so on. What he was determining was, "What are the relevant factors that must necessarily be in place for this new device to work sufficiently in the real world?" That is, he was asking about ingredients of a causal cake.

One relevant factor might be that the device must be dry, so no coffee can be spilled on it and no sweat dripped on it from nervous signatories. Another relevant factor might be that the Internet connection must be consistent and high bandwidth, so if a server crashes, we in London can't sign a document in Tokyo. Another relevant factor might be that all the component parts (including the rubber band that regulates the movement of the pen) must be intact. You would expect these, and others, as in figure III.1. The point is that the more of the necessary ingredients of the cake that you can determine, the more you'll be able to predict the effectiveness of the product, and what is required for the product to be effective.

Jeremy may get evidence, for instance, that, as in figure III.2.a, a properly functioning device plus a signatory who presses hard and does not sweat produces a reasonably good signature at the other end across even a long distance, so long as nothing untoward happens to the surface even after prolonged use of the machine and rubber band, independent of the quality of the Internet connection and the temperature. But if the signatory drips

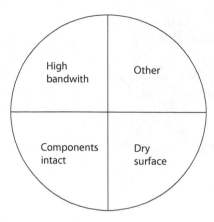

Figure III.1: A cake for LongPen

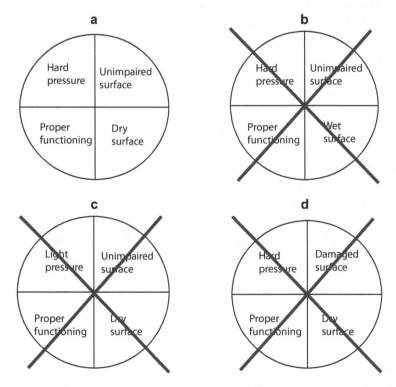

Figure III.2: More cakes for LongPen

sweat on the surface or presses lightly or messes up the surface, as in parts b, c, and d of figure III.2, it generally won't work. The first causal cake is positive for results; the others are not. And so on.

This list could have gotten longer and longer, and its components will subdivide. When it comes to deciding, you, like Jeremy, can do no more than hope that the list is complete enough and that the answers are as good as you can get. And then adjust your confidence about the prediction that the policy will work for you in accord with your confidence that you have all the support factors you need.

It is quite easy, even for non-financiers, to see that if you do all you can and still feel uneasy, you should not invest. Maybe you aren't confident enough that you have made a good list—because you can't understand the technology well and so can't see what might go wrong. Maybe you can't get enough good answers to the questions on the list, or can't see whether the answers are good or not. We think that, in the case of social policy, too, it is important to be honest enough to recognize that you can't always do a good job formulating and answering the questions that tell you whether the policy will work. And in social policy, too, you have to accept the consequences.

III.B.2 THINKING STEP-BY-STEP AND THINKING BACKWARDS

III.B.2.1 Sequences and Cakes

We keep reminding you that if you want your policy to work you had better think about whether you will have in place all the support factors necessary for it to do so. This demand can be daunting. How even do you get started on it?

Whether in an equation, prose, or a figure, you need to set out a list of the conditions that have to be met if the policy is to work here. The members of the list need not be set out in any particular order. It could, without loss, be randomly. Section III.B.1 suggested a strategy, pre-mortem, for identifying support factors, and that strategy involved no particular ordering of the factors. Whether LongPen would work depended on having a good Internet connection, not spilling coffee, and so. In this example, as in all our cake charts, the factors are not listed in any order; nor do they reflect any order in the process by which your policy is supposed to produce your desired outcome; and we did not impose any order on them in our thought. But in this section we suggest that ordering can help a great deal with the job of unearthing the list of support factors.

One way of thinking about support factors and contributions is analogous to how you describe the workings of a machine, such as an internal combustion engine. In describing the cycles of an Otto four-stroke gasoline engine, you talk about the Intake stroke, which has to precede the Compression stroke, which is succeeded by the Power stroke, and finally by the Exhaust stroke. Each of these is not only necessary for the result, but each has to happen as part of that sequence. It is no good just listing the four strokes in any old order.

Now, we are not saying that Society is a Machine. All that we take from this description is that it may be helpful when talking about how to identify support factors—the purpose of a horizontal search—to think in this step-by-step way. Nor do we say that all relevant factors will form part of a sequence. In some cases, it will not matter at all in what order things happen. Sometimes, it will matter a lot that this happens before that. So, as with all the strategies in III, the step-by-step strategy is offered as no more than one technique that may serve to show what conditions have to be satisfied, when, for a positive contribution to be made.

The technique is to think through how the policy leads to the desired outcome. Just what should happen, one step after another, starting with the policy and ending where you want to be? Things can go wrong at every step. And in just the ways we have been discussing. The salient factor at step 3 may not play the right causal role in your setting to produce what is necessary at step 4 in order to go on to step 5, and so on; or, maybe it can play the right causal role but the requisite support factors may not obtain then. Focusing on each step, one at a time, can help you to identify what needs to happen, and when, for the next step to follow. Gathering all these conditions together tells you what you need if the whole process is going to carry off successfully.

You can do this either by starting at the beginning with the policy implementation and ending with the targeted outcome, or by thinking backwards, from the outcome to the policy. It is often hard to think through the whole process. So sometimes it is a good idea to start at both ends and work toward the middle, hoping to get far enough to meet yourself there.

Both these strategies, step-by-step and thinking backwards, like the other strategies here in III, are useful ex ante, when you are concerned before you make the intervention to understand how it would work. But the same analysis works for ex post evaluation. If you did not get the result, what went wrong? There are two ways of approaching an answer to that. One is to see which of the support factors that you had identified beforehand were not after all present. The second is to check whether you had identified the right support factors, or failed to identify obstructive factors. A variant on the second is where you have not thought about support factors at all—say, because you thought that a Tennessee RCT was good enough—but failure makes you think about what support factors should have been present, such as enough teachers and classrooms. In all these cases, the structure of the evaluation analysis is the same as for the policy decision, but with the tense changed from the future to the past. We now set out three examples of this way of thinking.

III.B.2.2 Reducing Recidivism

Borrowing an example from Ray Pawson and Nick Tilley (1997: 103–14 and 169–75), suppose you consider setting up a campus in a particular prison to teach specific courses for male prisoners to reduce recidivism. Two central questions need to be answered. What is the causal process, step-by-step, that starts with the decision to fund the campus and ends with fewer prisoners returning to prison? What must be in place for each step to occur? You can accumulate a list of the steps necessary to achieve this and of the support factors necessary for each step in this process. In the end, *all* of them must be in place if the causal process is to run smoothly from start to finish.

There may, of course, be more than one route from cause to effect, more than one list, so that if support factors are missing for one or more steps on your first list, you may have them all for another list. But you need to have all the support factors needed along one entire route if you are to secure your desired outcome.

So, think the process through step-by-step. Just what must happen at each step to allow it to lead properly to the next and to play its required role in producing the outcome? Here's a sample answer sketch:

Step 1. You agree to fund it and appoint a manager who seems competent to negotiate and set it up properly. (There are such people available.)

Step 2. The manager negotiates an agreement with the prison governors. (It is not against prison rules and the governors are not opposed in principle.)

Step 3. The warden is approached and agrees. (Wardens are cooperative.)

Step 4. The warden, or the warden's delegate, and the manager figure out space for the classes and time. (It is not incompatible with prison schedule and rules; space is available.)

Step 5. Manager hires teachers. (There are competent willing people; they pass any regulations for being able to enter prison and interact with prisoners.)

Step 6. Students are recruited. (There is a way to make the program—and its possible benefits—known; enough prisoners will sign up; they will be ones who are able to attend; they will be ones able to reap the benefits, such as necessary background learning, reading skills, etc.)

Step 7. Classes begin. (The prisoners and instructors can be brought together at the prescribed times and places, which requires careful arrangements and security in the prison.)

Step 8. The instructors teach. (Necessary materials—white boards, projectors, handouts—are available.)

Step 9. The students study. (They have the right attitudes; they are not discouraged by other prisoners, prison guards, family, etc.; they have good enough time and study conditions; they have access to the necessary study materials.)

Step 10. The students take in the material. (They are competent to learn the kind of material being taught given the teaching methods used.)

Step 11. Students take credible exams. (It is possible to set up an exam scheme that has public credibility; it is possible to administer it.)

Step 12. Many pass.

Already you have a list of support factors that have to be in place if the policy is to work—from accessibility of transport to the prison for instructors to special security arrangements and time juggling of prison schedules to enable prisoners to attend lessons and study appropriately. And you are nowhere near to the desired outcome, which, after all, was not better educated prisoners but lower recidivism rates. What further factors must be in place if successful participation in this program is to decrease the chances of ending up back in prison? You have a start. But to be reasonably confident that the policy can help in reducing recidivism, you shall have to carry on, all the way to the end. Getting halfway there, or even 80 or 90% of the way, is of no use at all if it turns out that there is no way to put in place factors that are essential to complete the process.

III.B.2.3 Social Funds

Social funds are financed by the World Bank and other such agencies to channel resources to projects, typically schools and clinics.[3] One approach to evaluating the success of these projects is "theory based." That means that you do not just do experiments but you produce a defensible "theory"—a story or narrative—about just how the policy will achieve the intended outcome, and you look to see if the ingredients necessary at each stage were in place at the right time. So you set out the assumptions underlying the intervention in terms of the phased sequence of cause and effect that should lead to success. By seeing whether, and where, that sequence broke down, you can see why the project failed if it did. Or you have grounds for labeling it a success even though, after the project, things were overall worse than before because of the harmful effect of factors extraneous to the project.

Put like that, the analysis is ex post. But clearly, it is the same process to construct ex ante the sequence of cause and effect needed to achieve the objective, but with the tense changed. And, as before, the result may not have been, or may not be going to be, what you want for two kinds of reasons. You may have listed and sequenced the support factors correctly, but one or more may not have been present, or not at the right time. Or your list may be wrong.

Figure III.3 reproduces a diagram used by Soniya Carvalho and Howard White (2004: 145) to analyze what needs to be in place if a subproject (e.g., a school) is to produce sustainable benefits.

For example, see 4a in Figure III.3. If the school is to work and the work is to be sustainable, the community must contribute both to construction and maintenance. For that to happen, the community must have the capacity to implement and maintain investments. And what that means in practice can only be determined when the proposal has been formulated.

Similarly the table reproduced in table III.1 lists, under the column labeled "Theory," the factors that support the needed outcomes relating to subproject sustainability, and how you could find out whether those factors are likely to be in place. If there is to be a sense of community ownership, then, so the theory says, the school must be in accordance with community priorities. To assess whether that was the case, you have, for example, to see how much participation there was in formulating the project.

Assembling together all the ingredients supposed to be necessary, step-by-step, yields the causal cake of figure III.4 for achieving a contribution to subproject sustainability.

This case also shows, yet again, the need for vertical search to find just what can play the right causal role, which in turn can generate a need for different support factors than the ones required in other places. A nice example of a support factor in this case that you might not have thought of is that, for all the rhetoric about community, a successful project requires that there be a prime mover or champion. In Zambia, that is typically a head teacher; in Malawi, the chief. That prime mover must be someone who is "not afraid to enter offices." Then the project will get off the ground. But you have to know how the champion is effective. For example, this works best in rural areas. In cities, the chief lacks authority because he does not control the land. And some projects fail to be sustainable because there is nobody

Figure III.4: A cake for social funds subproject sustainability

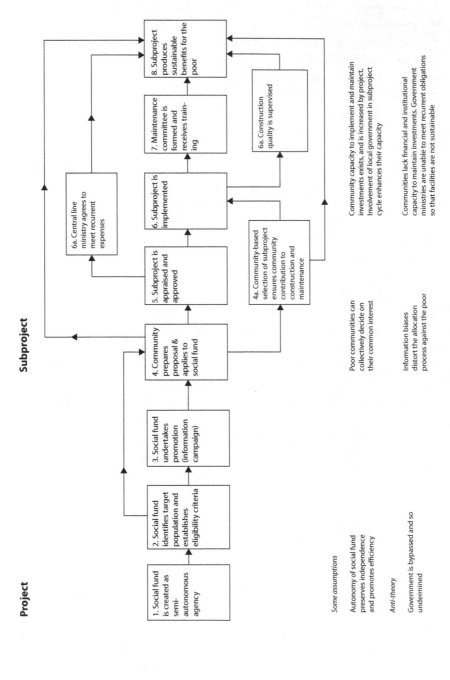

Project

Subproject

1. Social fund is created as semi-autonomous agency

2. Social fund identifies target population and establishes eligibility criteria

3. Social fund undertakes promotion (information campaign)

4. Community prepares proposal & applies to social fund

5. Subproject is appraised and approved

6. Subproject is implemented

7. Maintenance committee is formed and receives training

8. Subproject produces sustainable benefits for the poor

6a. Central line ministry agrees to meet recurrent expenses

6a. Construction quality is supervised

4a. Community-based selection of subproject ensures community contribution to construction and maintenance

Some assumptions

Autonomy of social fund preserves independence and promotes efficiency

Poor communities can collectively decide on their common interest

Community capacity to implement and maintain investments exists, and is increased by project. Involvement of local government in subproject cycle enhances their capacity

Anti-theory

Government is bypassed and so undermined

Information biases distort the allocation process against the poor

Communities lack financial and institutional capacity to maintain investments. Government ministries are unable to meet recurrent obligations so that facilities are not sustainable

Figure III.3: How to produce sustainable benefits. From Carvalho and White 2004: 145.

Table III.1 FRAMEWORK FOR ANALYSIS OF SUBPROJECT SUSTAINABILITY

Theory	Assumptions	Data Required to Test the Assumptions
The invitation of proposals from communities ensures that the chosen investments reflect top community priorities, which engenders community ownership	(i) "Community" is a meaningful construct; (ii) communities hear about the offer of funds; (iii) subprojects eligible for social fund financing are consistent with community priorities; (iv) the community feels ownership of the investment.	(i) Extent and nature of participation (who participates and how much they partici-pate); (ii) extent of agreement in the community that the subproject chosen is a priority investment; (iii) consistency of the social fund subproject menu with community priorities.
Community ownership results in willingness to take responsibility for operating and maintaining the investment.	(i) Community members are aware of, and accept their obligations regarding operations and maintenance, (ii) formal or informal systems for monitoring and enforcement of community contributions are in place to prevent free riding.	(i) Awareness of responsibilities among community members; (ii) perception among community members about whether burden is fairly shared; (iii) penalties for free-riders.
Those responsible for operations and maintenance have the ability to effectively discharge their operations and maintenance functions.	(i) Those responsible have the necessary financial, technical, and institutional wherewithal/skills to meet their operations and maintenance obligations.	(i) Financial, technical, and institutional capability of community members and other intermediaries to undertake operations and maintenance.
Formal assurances improve the likelihood of government support.	(i) Government responsibilities are clearly identified and agreed upon at project identification/design; (ii) mechanisms exist for government contributions to materialize; (iii) governement has the resources to provide the promised contribution.	(i) Government's budgetary, technical, and financial capacity to meet its obligations; (ii) government's willingness to meet these obligations.
The social fund agency's design and monitoring ensure sustainable investments.	(i) Social fund agency's appraisal capacities are adequate and it rejects proposals that are not sustainable; (ii) social fund agency provides adequate technical designs and support to community, including training; (iii) social fund agency puts in place effective mechanisms to ensure follow-up (including operations and maintenance).	(i) The adequacy and appropriateness of the social fund agency's institutional, financial, and technical arrangements for sustainability.

(continued)

Table III.1 (*Continued*)

Theory	Assumptions	Data Required to Test the Assumptions
Demonstration effects	(i) Social fund approach and procedures are superior and suitable for adoption elsewhere; (ii) there is knowledge about these approaches/procedures among government agencies.	(i) Extent to which social funds successfully demonstrate new approaches; (ii) extent of contact and coordination between the social fund and government agencies; (iii) evidence of government agencies embracing social fund procedues.
Learning-by-doing effects	(i) Social fund involves government agencies in decision-making/planning or uses government agencies as subproject sponsoring entities.	(i) Extent of involvement of government agencies in social fund decision-mkaing/planning processes; (ii) extent of adoption of social fund approaches by government agency.
Competition effects	(i) Governement agency is able to detect that it is in competition with the social fund agency; (ii) government agency is able to reform and meet challenge.	(i) Measures of efficiency (i.e., extent to which existing resources begin to be better used); (ii) extent of actual or likely shifts in the roles and responsibilities of government agencies.
Demand effects	(i) Communities increase their demand for governement services; (ii) government agency is in a position to respond.	(i) Level and nature of community demands; (ii) extent of government response to demands
Side effects		
Resource allocation effects	(i) Social fund and other agencies compete for staff/resources.	(i) Movement of staff from government to social fund agency.
Systemic budget effects	(i) Social fund resources are off-budget and they undermine accountability, reduce fiscal prudence, and distort the budgetary allocation process.	(i) National budget; (ii) procedures for budget accountability.
Decentralization effects	(i) Government is attempting decentralization; (ii) social fund strengthens investment planning/resource allocation; (iii) social fund undermines investment planning/resource allocation.	(i) Decentralization policy; (ii) nature of local government investment planning/resource allocation process; (iii) relationship between the social fund agency and local government

Source: From Carvalho and White 2004: 152.

who has a direct interest or position to keep them going. The head teacher wants the school to continue to succeed. But there are no "roadmasters" or "watermasters" to keep road or water projects going. So no champion.

III.B.2.4 Feedback Loops: An Example from Child Welfare Policy

Policies, even good ones, can figure in negative cakes, right alongside the positive ones. The negative cakes will certainly diminish the good effects of the policy, and can even, if they are prevalent enough or strong enough, outweigh the good effects. You can sometimes unearth the negative effects by thinking through the causal process from beginning to end, step-by-step, as we have been describing. This can be particularly important if any of the causal stages in between are self-reinforcing, so that the outcomes, negative or positive, escalate over time. One good example of where worries about negative cakes and self-reinforcement have arisen is in the UK's recent Munro Review of Child Protection (Munro 2011). The analysis from the Review is set out in the diagram in figure III.5.

The Review's own version of the story can be seen in Appendix II. Here is a short version: the original policy was intended to improve welfare outcomes in children and young people (CYP) by providing stricter guidelines for what social workers must do in dealing with children and families and by better monitoring of what they are doing. This involved ensuring that specific mandated facts about the family and the child were ascertained and recorded properly and that various required meetings took place. But this policy itself, the Review argues, can have serious negative effects on child outcomes alongside the intended positive effects. How so? Through various negative feedback loops.

Two negative loops were specifically described in the Review: R1 and R2 in figure III.5. Both start off in the same way. If you increase the amount of prescription that you impose on social workers, you can reduce their sense of satisfaction and self-esteem. In R1, this increases staff sickness and absence rates; in R2, it increases staff turnover rates. Both these effects can easily result in an increase in average social worker caseload, which then leads to social workers spending less time with the children and young people and their families. This in turn reduces the quality of the social workers' relationships with the children and the families, which then reduces the quality of the outcomes. So the policy may produce bad unintended consequences. Worse, these negative effects can become amplified via the feedback loops. When the outcomes are regularly too unsatisfactory, this reduces social workers' sense of self-esteem and personal responsibility, and the whole negative cycle is set in motion again.

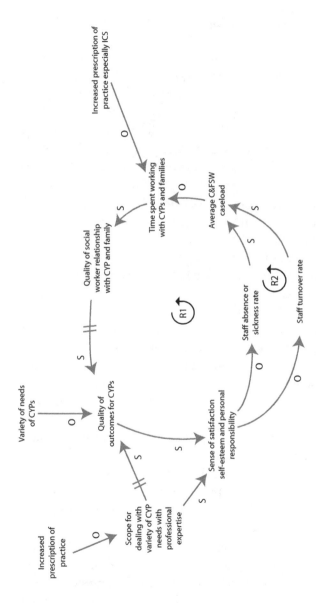

An arrow linking variable A to variable B should be read as 'a change in the value of A produces a change in the value of B'. The qualitative nature of the link is indicated by a 'link polarity'. These should be read as:

- 'S': the variables move in the same direction *ceteris paribus*, so a change in variable A produces a change in variable B in the same direction: if A goes up, B goes up.

- 'O': the variables move in the opposite direction *ceteris paribus*, so a change in variable A produces a change in variable B in the opposite direction: if A goes up, B goes down.

- double bars on a link indicate a particularly long delay in the causal connection.

Note that the link polarity says nothing about the size, or quantity of the change. The indication of the effect is qualitative only. Moreover, there is no presumption of a linear relationship between the two variables.

Figure III.5: The impact of increased prescription of social work practice. From Munro 2011: 136.

We reproduce the causal loop diagram from the Munro Review because it shows you another of the benefits of thinking through the policy process step-by-step: you may discover causal loops that will magnify the outcomes over time. Drawing the picture does not tell you whether it is the right picture. Nor does it tell you what the support factors are for each stage to lead to the next, nor whether they are present, nor how to find that out. It tells you what the salient factor is at each step that is expected to play a causal role in producing the next step. And it contains no quantities, only the direction of effect. Its big advantage is that it reminds you of the possibility of negative effects alongside the positive ones, and it reminds you that the causal process may not be linear. Feedback loops may unexpectedly enhance the outcome, either for the good or for the bad.

III.B.3 IT WORKS. BY MEANS OF WHAT?

III.B.3.1 Example: Car Theft and CCTV

Chapter II.B illustrated how hunting for the right kind of description at the right level of abstraction can help you to find both a policy variable that can play a positive causal role in your setting and also to identify what its requisite support factors are. Here we shall give another extended illustration plus a strategy for this kind of hunt. The strategy is to ask: "If it is to work, by what means will it do so?" What abstract feature that can generally be relied on is being called into play? Here is a case study to show what we mean. The study is taken directly from the work of Ray Pawson and Nick Tilley (1997), which we recommend to the reader in its entirety.[4]

If you are thinking about the effectiveness of putting CCTV cameras into parking lots to reduce crime, it would be a big help to have a story about how and why that is meant to work. As Pawson and Tilley point out, "There is nothing about CCTV in car parks which intrinsically inhibits car crime" (1997: 78). If CCTV does inhibit car crime, it must be because it is a case of something that can play this causal role. So we ask, "In virtue of what does CCTV inhibit car crime?"

This looks a bit banal. Of course, it works by getting thieves on camera, so that they are arrested and charged, there and then, by the police arriving and catching them. Call this:

  a. Caught in the act.

More thought suggests other ways that it might work. The thieves may expect to get away from the scene of the crime. But if they know that their photo is on camera and they may be tracked down later, they may be deterred. Call this:

b. You've been framed.

These first two examples make you realize that if you are to bet on even these two simple accounts of what it is about CCTV that gives it the capacity to prevent car crime, you have to think about what is needed to make them operate. That is, you have to think about what support factors are needed. For *caught in the act*, you need there to be police near enough to make the arrest at once. For *you've been framed*, CCTV evidence has to be allowable in court, or at least believed by the prospective thieves to be so.

You have a policy—put in CCTV cameras—and you have to decide whether it will work in this parking lot. To do that, you have to be clear about what general, more abstract feature CCTV calls into play that makes it work; for example, *caught in the act* or *you've been framed*. Unless you know which you are relying on, you don't know whether absence of police matters, because you have not identified whether prompt police presence is a support factor. Because the policy does not work of itself, but has to work *somehow*, you cannot just, by considering the policy, know whether it will work.

Once you have answered the question about what allows CCTV to work, you are led to questions about what support factors are needed. And then, of course, to whether they are likely to be present. You have to answer all these questions correctly to get an effectiveness conclusion. This section is about thinking about the first question. But answering it correctly can be a big help in answering the second.

Sometimes, the first answer helps you answer yes/no questions. Should the cameras be visible? No, if you are relying on *caught in the act*. The longer the thieves think that they are unobserved, the better the chance that the police will get there. Yes, if you are relying on *you've been framed*. The clearer it is that they will be identified, the more likely that they will be deterred.

The visible/invisible example shows nicely how little you can get from evidence that it worked there, of which an RCT is one source. You propose that CCTV be put in this parking lot because it worked there. The police say, "Do we need to think about how we provide rapid response?" You can't answer that unless you know how to answer the question about what allows it to work. If they say that they can't provide rapid response, do you give up? Or do you say that you will make the cameras visible and rely on *you've been framed*? What if the lawyer says that CCTV evidence is not admissible in court and all the car thieves know that? If you don't give up then, why not? What other account of what allows it to work do you have in mind?

RCTs don't help with any of this. At best, they give you the positive starting point that in that place there were the right answers to your questions, so you might think what those answers might have been. But it will be a hard grind to get to the conclusion that this policy will be effective here.

III.B.3.2 More on CCTV and Some General Lessons

Here are three lists that show what you might have to think about when you are deciding on the effectiveness here of CCTV cameras. It is not necessary fully to understand it, let alone critique it.[5]

a. Caught in the act
b. You've been framed
c. Nosy parker
d. Effective deployment
e. Publicity
f. Time for crime
g. Memory jogging
h. Appeal to the cautious

And for each of these, you have to consider the context.

 i. Criminal clustering
 ii. Style of usage
iii. Lie of the land
iv. Alternative targets
 v. Resources
vi. Surveillance culture

Which require the following lines of investigation:

1. Conviction capability
2. Criminal opportunities
3. Location
4. Temporal pattern
5. Publicity mechanism

We reproduce in Appendix III the full version of these lists, which makes clearer the content of each of its members. We use it not to provide a checklist, like a preflight routine, to make sure that you cover everything, but to illustrate one of our central arguments, that deliberation, because it is open-ended, can produce a very long list. And that, although it is hard to do well, and there can be no chance of doing it perfectly or conclusively, it is a process that you have to use all the time in thinking about whether what you propose will work. Thinking about the questions we set is open-ended because it is a process of thinking about relevance.

The case study and this list illustrate several features of the factors by which a given policy might work:

1. It is not obvious what should be in the list. You have to think.
2. The considerations that make you put a feature on the list are very various. A controlled experiment comparing parking lots with, and parking lots without, CCTV is a rare, and bad, source of ideas about identifying these more abstractly described features.
3. For any of these general, abstract features to operate, many other conditions have to be in place. *Caught in the act* only works if the police arrive quickly enough. The wall around the parking lot must be too high to jump. Deterrence only works if CCTV evidence is acceptable in court, unlike wiretapping evidence.
4. Much of the information you need comes from background knowledge. One question is whether the parking lot is easy to get out of. If it is surrounded by an 8-foot wall, then thieves will find it harder to get away before the police arrive. So that favors the bet on installing the cameras. In this particular case, therefore, you have to know whether there is such a wall. But you also have to know that thieves cannot jump such walls, and for that, whether you acknowledge it consciously or not, you are relying on generalizations about physics, the human body, how unlikely it is that the thief will be 7-feet tall or, just know that most people can't jump 8-foot walls. You don't need high theory to tell you that, nor experiments with differing heights of walls.
5. But some need more work. You know that deterrence won't work if CCTV detection is believed never to lead to conviction. But you don't know without inquiry what the legal and evidential problems are with CCTV evidence, nor what prospective thieves believe about it. You have to find out.
6. Of the several kinds of facts you need to find out if you are to decide to put in CCTV cameras, some apply to all contexts—for example, whether CCTV evidence is admissible—though even then contexts will differ in a relevant way if the clarity of the image is evidentially important. Some are very particular—the height of the wall is irrelevant if it is an underground parking lot. How you establish the facts that you have otherwise decided to be relevant varies a lot. You can look at the wall. You have to ask a lawyer about the admissibility of CCTV evidence.

III.B.4 DECISIONS USING QUICK EXIT TREES

III.B.4.1 Quick Exit Trees

Decision trees are a familiar device to help with figuring out what to do. Our simple decision trees are "quick exit" trees.[6] In the first instance, they allow you to eliminate alternative polices quickly. The trees start off with a fork at which a question is asked. Two branches lead off from the fork, one branch of which leads to NO, the other to YES. The NO is a dead end. Suppose the first question is "Have we got the money to do this?" If the answer is NO, you stop. If it is YES, you go on down the branch to the next question. And so on.

If the answer is NO, some decision trees, not ours, lead into another question, such as "Could we get some?" and then into further alternatives. If one of those generates a YES, then you could be led back to the end of the YES branch of the first fork. And so on. There is no end to the complexity of decision trees, as the wide variety of available software shows. But the quick exit decision tree is simple. It has the following characteristics:

1. If fully completed, it provides an unequivocal answer to the question, "Will this policy be effective here?"
2. To do that, it sets out all the conditions that have to be fulfilled for the policy to make the contribution you want, both those about causal roles and those about support factors.
3. These conditions are set out by asking a question at each fork—is this condition met?—with only two branches: YES/NO.
4. If the answer is NO, you go no further. The question has been answered. The policy won't work. A necessary condition has not been met.
5. The decision tree represents only one cake, one set of conditions sufficient for a contribution. There will, of course, be other cakes, represented by other decision trees, that offer a route to a contribution to the effect you want. Some of these will provide an answer to the same question about this policy, because they contain this policy as an ingredient. Even if the answer to the first decision tree is NO, there may be another decision tree, with different, but not necessarily all different, components, that shows another route whereby the policy can make a contribution. Others will show a successful route in answer to a quite different question, for example, "Will this other policy work?"

Thinking like this, and using this simple quick exit decision tree structure, makes you concentrate on identifying which conditions are not fulfilled, which forks lead to a NO. This makes these trees a good tool early in deliberation when you still have a lot of policies under consideration. You only need one NO to reject a policy and move on to consider the next. The quick exit structure encourages you to look for, and identify early, necessary conditions that will appear in many, or maybe all, cakes where your policy variable appears. It is no good thinking through all the factors needed to make a youth crime policy work if all policies need money, and at a time of cuts there is no money for new policies.

Quick exit trees fulfill this same function when you are concentrating on a single policy, and so are useful later in deliberation as well. You don't have to undertake the daunting task of getting all the necessary factors listed before you look to see whether the policy will work. Nor do you have to consider factors in any special order. As soon as you hit a necessary factor that won't be there for you (or that you won't be able to obtain), you know the policy is unlikely to work. That's the beauty of thinking in terms of necessary factors.

There is, of course, a more positive use. If you have carried on long enough and have covered all the conditions necessary for your policy to work, with YES at every node, and you can be reasonably confident that you have done so, then you have good reason to believe your policy will work here in your circumstances.

III.B.4.2 Example: Jobs for Problem Drug Users

Here is a real example. What it shows is that deciding whether the policy would work appears to require identifying and verifying the presence of a long list of conditions. But that work could have been bypassed if at the start one key condition had been identified that showed that the policy would never work.

In Britain, as elsewhere, there is an ambition to adopt policies that take people off welfare into work. This is partly to save money, but also to give them a better life as part of mainstream society. One class of welfare recipients is problem drug users (PDUs) defined as those dependent on heroin or crack cocaine. Against this background, the United Kingdom Drug Policy Commission (UKDPC) set about looking at what was needed to get PDUs off welfare into work and reintegrated into society (UKDPC 2008).

The proposed welfare to work policies—called "Work Ready" policies—included then, as now, the idea that claimants be required to take action to get a job, and, if they fail to do enough, then benefits should be withdrawn. The belief is that the fear of loss of benefits will motivate people to take action that will lead to them getting a job. This approach is based on a number of assumptions about why PDUs are remaining on benefits and not getting jobs. And these in turn suggest what assumptions must be true and what support factors must be in place if the policies are to work.

First, that PDUs are in need of being motivated to work and that this can be done. That may be by the threat of losing benefits. Or, perhaps more likely, it may be otherwise, if coercion is a poor way of motivating people. In any case, they don't have to be economic man, perfectly rational, but they must have some capacity for thinking ahead, imagining alternative futures, keeping one of them in mind as a way forward. But addiction to drugs involves a focus on drugs above anything else.

Second, that they will be equipped by, for example, training, and enabled by, for example, having accommodation, to take up and keep a long-term job. Taking these and other support factors together, you can set up a simple decision tree like that in figure III.6. You then set about finding evidence for the fulfillment of these conditions, which will be hard work.

We said that the decision tree is simple, and it is. Answering YES or NO is bipolar. You can't, in this framework, accommodate answers like "Their drug use is quite well controlled." Put another way, the thresholds are for

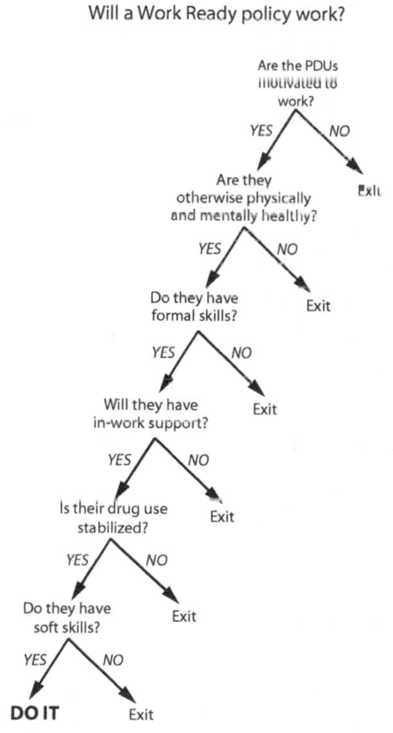

Will a Work Ready policy work?

Figure III.6: A quick exit decision tree for "Work Ready" policies

saying YES or NO. If they are clear, as they have to be, they will score 49 (or whatever) as failure and 51 as success, no "matter of degree."

Quick exit decision trees do not prioritize one condition over another. Order is irrelevant, except that the sooner you hit on a NO, the sooner you can stop. For its positive use, the decision tree remains just a way of setting out a list. One way of prioritizing is by looking at timing, as we suggested in the step-by-step technique. (Remember, the strategies we describe can be complementary—you can use more than one of them on the same problem. And none is comprehensive—so you may need to use more than one.) Maybe, before you do any training, you have to stabilize drug use. That is a precondition. It should come high up the page if you are looking for possible quick exits.

In the UKDPC's work, the moment of truth came from part of the research that had been undertaken because of a suspicion that it might matter a lot. The research suggested that very few employers want to take on PDUs even if all the conditions in the decision tree in figure III.6 are fulfilled. Even if reducing benefits caused PDUs seriously to seek employment, and training equipped them for available jobs, they would not get jobs. Employers would not believe that the processes designed to make PDUs fit for work would make them employable people, given a history of irresponsibility, often criminality, and a continuing need for in-work support and risk of slipping. In particular, they do not believe that a successful methadone regime constitutes stabilization of drug use. In our simple decision tree framework, this insight would have made you put "Will employers take them on?" into the tree. And it's good luck if you manage to put it in at the top and find out the right answer. So that when the answer is NO, you stop. And you never look at the rest of this tree.

So that is what the quick decision tree gives you. It can save, at least for the time being, all the hard work needed to collect the evidence the rest of this decision tree requires. That is all it does. But that should lead naturally to thinking about what you can do about the NO answer to "Will employers take them on?" That will be hard work too. But at least you can park this decision tree, and the work it requires, until you have seen whether that NO can be turned into a YES. And you can save the money that putting a Work Ready policy into effect might have wasted.

III.B.4.3 French Food in Pubs

Here is another example. Again it is real, or rather, based on reality. But in this case the crucial necessary condition (analogous to "Will employers take them on?") was satisfied, and the policy went ahead.

Should we open pubs?

Will the menu appeal
to customers?

YES   NO

Is it in the right
price bracket?   Exit

YES   NO

Can we run a pub
alongside a restaurant?   Exit

YES   NO

Do our staff have the
right experience?   Exit

YES   NO

Have we got
the money?   Exit

YES   NO

DO IT   Exit

Figure III.7: A quick exit decision tree for opening pubs

A business running a chain of French restaurants wondered whether some version of what they were doing in restaurants would work in pubs. They devised a somewhat simpler, lower price offer. They then had to decide whether a policy of entering the market with this offer would work. Again, a decision tree can be drawn up, as in figure III.7.

And in this case too there is an important necessary condition missing. Late in the process, the company realized that the market in freeholds and leaseholds of pubs was changing. Institutional investors were pushing up prices, so the question "Can we get the right pubs at the right price?" had to be dealt with. And, like the question "Will employers take them on?" it deserves priority. If you can't get the right properties, the answers to the other questions don't matter. So you ought to promote this question to the top. In this case, the rise in price did not generate a NO, so they got to YES DO IT.

III.B.4.4 Cautions

For quick exit trees to lead to a sure NO, it is not enough for there to be a factor from one cake missing. In addition, the factor has to be a trump in the sense of II.A.7. Positive trumps are propositions that, if true, make it certain that the policy will be effective. Support factors do not matter. Negative trumps similarly make sure that the policy will not work, and the presence or absence of other support factors does not matter. A trump does not only make this cake fail. It also makes any cake with that policy in it fail, whatever other support factors you think up. If you can't buy pubs, you can't start a pub business. So don't think about how you might do it otherwise than how you first envisaged it. If employers won't employ PDUs, don't bother with other ways of making PDUs Fit for Work, because nothing can overcome that obstacle.

Spotting that a factor is a trump is a step on from spotting that it is a necessary ingredient in a particular cake. One way of spotting that is to see that it has sabotaged one cake, and the next . . . until you realize that its importance is much greater than you thought—it has no substitutes, and there are no alternative cakes that work.

Even when the trump is real, you may wish to think about how you might neutralize it. You should certainly not waste time on a training program for PDUs if employers will not employ them, if in that sense they can never be made Fit for Work. But that analysis should lead to thinking about how employers might come, for example, to take another view of methadone regimes. So the dead end may be only pro tem.

The danger with quick exit trees is that they may license premature identification of factors lethal to the project of, for example, dealing with PDUs. Particularly if there is prejudice against the project (why spend money on druggies?), or it is expensive, or hard to think about, it is a relief to say that it is ruled out from the start—"I agree with you but we will never get the money, so let's not waste time." This is the opposite of the magic bullet and must be guarded against similarly. As always, you have to be careful. But that is the human condition. We can always be too quick, too biased, too ignorant. What matters is, as always, that the probability of your effectiveness conclusion is no higher than the probability of your premises, which in this case are the claims that back the NO and give you a quick exit.

That said, it is a good idea to be alert to the possibility that you can identify early on a factor that will be fatal to almost any way of getting the policy to contribute to your desired effect, and our simple quick exit decision trees aim to help with that. As with all our strategies, we have no way of immunizing users from the consequences of error or misuse.

PART FOUR

RCTs, Evidence-Ranking Schemes, and Fidelity

CHAPTER IV.A

Where We Are and Where We Are Going

The reality of much contemporary evidence-based policy and practice as it is, or is meant to be, carried out today is that good evidence for a policy has come to mean a good RCT, an RCT that shows that the policy has worked. That is what the evidence-ranking schemes tell you.

In Parts II and III we concentrated on how, in the light of our theory, we recommend that you should set about identifying key facts you need beyond this for effectiveness decisions. These key facts are about the causal role that the policy has to play and the support factors that it needs. They are what you need to know if you are to answer the how question: "How did the policy work and how can I expect it to work here?" We elaborated the notions of horizontal and vertical search, and we suggested four strategies that may help to carry out those searches. In the course of this, we have barely mentioned RCTs or evidence-ranking schemes or fidelity.

Here in Part IV we go back to contemporary practice and look, in light of our theory and recommendations, at what you can get from RCTs, from the evidence-ranking schemes that privilege them, and from the advice to be faithful to just what worked elsewhere, if you are concerned to identify and confirm these key facts. Unsurprisingly, the answer is "not much" and certainly not as much as contemporary practice assumes. That's because, as we noted in I.B, RCTs—like any other method for warranting "it worked somewhere"—are only a starting point on the long road to predicting that a policy will work for you.

CHAPTER IV.B

⟨∿⟩

What Are RCTs Good For?

IV.B.1 WHAT'S GOOD ABOUT RCTS?

RCTs are privileged in most evidence use guides and by most warehouses that vet policies following their advice. You are told that if you are to choose a policy in the specific context of your school or town, you should choose one that is backed by the best evidence. And the best evidence is an RCT, or better, a positive verdict from a systematic review or a meta-analysis of good RCTs.

In IV.C we give a representative list of agencies that vet and warehouse policies. But for illustration we mention here the Campbell and Cochrane Collaborations, which are volunteer organizations that review social and medical polices, respectively, and the What Works Clearing House, sponsored by the US Department of Education to vet educational policies. All provide a list giving you the interventions that are shown by RCTs (typically) to have worked. You then choose the intervention that suits your desired outcome, because . . . Because why? Because the studies have been vetted and certified to provide evidence that, as the saying goes, "it works."

First let us set out what is good and impressive about RCTs. They do in the ideal—that is, if the study procedures, like masking, randomizing, and placebo control, succeed in securing all the requisite assumptions—prove that this policy caused that outcome, there, in that population, that it played a positive causal role there. This is what the RCT Argument from I.B.5.2 shows. In Tennessee, reducing class size contributed to better reading scores. In two Zambian hospitals, introducing co-trimoxazole contributed to increased survival rates in HIV positive children (Chintu et al. 2004).[1] If properly done, they can provide confidence that there was the difference indicated between those who received the treatment and those who did not, and that the treatment played a causal role in producing this difference. It was not, for example, an accident or due to some cause held in common by the policy and the outcome.

RCTs produce this remarkable result because they are special. We say that they *clinch* causal conclusions: if the assumptions of the study design are met, a positive result (in the words of our theory chapter, a "positive treatment effect") deductively implies that the policy under test causes the outcome under investigation in some study members. You can see this by looking back to the RCT Argument.

Note that we say *if* the assumptions of the study design are met. All designs, not just RCTs, have assumptions that must be met to ensure they deliver reliable results. And among these there will always be assumptions about other causal relations. For instance, RCTs require that other causes that affect the outcome be distributed evenly in treatment and control groups; Bayes' nets methods, which we described briefly in I.B.5.3, generally assume that all omitted causes are probabilistically independent of one another; and this is typical in causal modeling in econometrics as well. Hence, the slogan, "No causes in, no causes out."

What is special about RCTs is that they are *self-validating*. The study design itself provides warrant for the assumptions required to underwrite the reliability of the results, without the need to import background causal knowledge from elsewhere. All the causes of the outcome other than the one under test are to be distributed in the same way in the treatment and control groups. But you do not need to know what these are in order to have some confidence that this requirement is satisfied. Masking, random assignment, and placebo control are supposed to satisfy this requirement for you.

So RCTs can produce highly trustworthy causal claims—claims that you have good reason to have confidence in. But they only secure the starting point on the long road from "it works there" to "it will work here." In stressing this we are not primarily concerned with the wide variety of more or less serious criticisms that can be made of many actual RCTs. For example, the effectiveness of small classes in Tennessee cannot have been established by double masked studies—everyone must have known who was getting what treatment. Our concern is with the relevance of these claims, supposing that they are technically well founded. What are they evidence for? You need trustworthy claims that are relevant to the policy. Showing that a claim is very likely true goes no way to showing that it is relevant to the truth of your policy effectiveness prediction.

One of the attractions of RCTs is that you can prove what caused the outcome without understanding how it happened. You put the drug in, and out comes a cure. But you get no idea from the RCT how that happened.

You can ignore the effect of other factors, including what we have called the "support factors." More strongly, you not only need not know what might be the effect of these factors, you don't even have to know what they are, or even whether there are any. And nobody has to know the answer to these questions. It is not that you; the policy maker, can take a free ride and have confidence that this caused that despite your ignorance, without wondering how it happened, because somebody knows. Nobody has to know how it happened.

For us, answering the "how" question means learning the key facts that have to be true for the policy intervention to work here, in your situation. When you focus just on RCTs, you are saying that this question can be made not to matter. This is how most of us treat machines most of the time. We just want to know that the machine will work. If the car gets me there, that's all that I am interested in. I do not have to ask the "how" question and would not understand the answer if I asked. So far, so like an RCT. But machines are special. Even if 99% of users never ask the how question, the how question has certainly got an answer, and a very precise answer. The company that developed the machine knows exactly how it works. And they did not find out how it worked; they did not discover it. They invented it, and its structure is like that because they made it so.

And it has typically been developed so that the question "if it worked there, will it work here?" has become redundant before it went into production. If it hadn't, it wouldn't have gone into production at all. It embodies configurations chosen precisely because the same configurations will be effective in a very large number of contexts. A great deal of care is taken to ensure that there are many contexts in which the machine works. Whereas an RCT only tells you that the policy did play a positive causal role there and that support factors were indeed present there, but not that either of these will be true if you implement it here, a machine is set up so that you know that its parts will play the right causal roles, with the right support factors, here, there, and everywhere that it is supposed to perform.

IV.B.2 ANSWERING THE HOW QUESTION

Our single most important message is that the conditions necessary for you not to have to worry about the key facts that have to be fulfilled in the design and use of machines of general application cannot be relied on to be satisfied in most settings where social policy is meant to operate. How does the policy produce the intended outcome? For successful social policy you cannot avoid answering this how question. And there is nothing odd about doing that.

Physicists knows how to build shields to block out the possible effects of any factors that might have been missed. But they also use strong background knowledge of what other causes may be operating. In medicine, there is a strong background presumption, often not explicit, that for the purposes of many medical interventions, human beings are all much the same in the relevant respects, except perhaps for obvious ones, like age, sex, and other illnesses. This notion of putative commonality in turn depends on the idea that there are quite high-level generalizations to be had from science that can without challenge be applied to all human beings. Or at least that is the default position, to be questioned only if there is a particular reason to do so. It is a rebuttable presumption, but rebuttal is hard.

This idea, of what science can provide for you if you are deciding what is going to happen, comes up in what might be thought the center of RCT territory, given the requirements of the Food and Drug Administration and others, that is, the development of new drugs. But the fact that, at the end, you have to do an RCT for approval is misleading about what you need to have in developing a new drug. Particularly given the costs of RCTs, the only drugs that get to be tested are those that there are very good reasons to think will work widely. And the good reasons come from the background knowledge that science provides. The fact is that RCTs come at the end, when you have already decided that it will probably work, here and maybe anywhere, that it works, that it fits with your categories. To know that this is a good bet, you have to have thought about causal roles and support factors. That is most easily done when you have some good generalizations about how things work. That is what science gives you—good background knowledge. So answering the how question is made easier in science by background knowledge of how things work.

A central problem in social policy is that there is little equivalent background knowledge. And an RCT doesn't help much. It doesn't help much to be told, tantalizingly, that the policy can play a causal role here if only its causal role is the same as there and the support factors for it to do so are in place here, but I'm not giving you any grounds for supposing that the causal role will be the same nor any clue what those support factors are.

We know that most all cars work much the same, and that you need gas to make them work. In that case, you have the good reasons derived from the history of the design of the machine to believe this. But it is another thing to say you have good reasons to believe that this school is like that school, as that machine is like this. It is that kind of optimism that allows the US Department of Education to say, almost as an aside "in school settings similar to yours" as though there is very likely to be a common causal role, and as though the support factors are very likely to be present in your school unless there is clear reason to suppose the contrary, like the move from well-off suburban schools to those in disadvantaged areas of the inner city (USDE 2003: 10).

So privileging RCTs is like saying that an RCT tells you that you can use this machine pretty much anywhere without lifting the hood, routinely. And people who have not got much insight into its workings can just use the machine without thinking. Because millions of cars have been used in millions of different sets of circumstances, it would be absurd to ask whether my new VW is likely to work in France, or in three years' time. That is because confidence that cars work in a large range of circumstances has been made routine by repeated success. And people who know nothing at all about mechanical engineering would be right to conclude that their VW would start in the morning because of the well-documented evidence that VWs almost always start. And it is not of much day-to-day interest to know that very rarely, in very odd circumstances, it doesn't, or that there may be circumstances that we haven't thought of where it won't.

But even with machines, there is a lot hidden behind the assumption that it will work here and now, and in rare but sometimes horrible cases that assumption is wrong. The 1986 Space Shuttle Challenger disaster occurred because an O-ring seal failed at lift off, leading to the breakup of the vehicle (PC 1986: ch. 4, §70.6). Among other things, it was assumed that O-rings would operate properly even in temperatures 15 degrees lower than the next coldest previous launch. So the reassuring record of previous reliability was not enough. The conditions in the here and now were outside the range.

Our central question is how often you can proceed with negligible risk of failure, on the assumption that it will work here because it has worked there. That is a good assumption for VWs, both because there is long experience of success and you, or at least the engineers, know how it works. Our suggestion is that in social policy the assumption is heroic, and you had better be careful in making it, because typically neither you nor the engineers have much understanding of how it may work. In social policy, to get confidence, you have to try to understand what is going on—what is the shared role that makes it work in these places, and what concrete factor will exemplify this role here, in the place you are going next. And will that new locale have in place the support factors that it needs? To answer these questions, you need horizontal and vertical thinking.

IV.B.3 PILING ON THE RCTs

Social policy typically does not proceed by repeated testing in a wide variety of circumstances. But maybe, even practicalities apart, that is a mistake. Opponents of the demand to identify causal roles and support factors ask, not for horizontal and vertical search, but for more and more RCTs. That's usually because they do not want to trust any background knowledge nor any theory in the social, economic, or biomedical sciences, neither high "scientific" theory nor low folk theory. We agree that more RCTs, especially across a variety of circumstances, can be a big help in warranting effectiveness predictions. But their evidential relevance will always be indirect, by warranting claims that the policy worked somewhere, or in a number of different somewheres.

And it will be conditional. Recall the basic Effectiveness Argument outlined in I.B.7.5. Seeing the same policy work there, there, and there again can provide evidence that it can play a causal role broadly, perhaps even broadly enough to cover here, and that the support factors necessary for it to do so are widespread. But working in lots of somewheres is only evidentially relevant to "it will work here" conditional on other assumptions. If these other assumptions are not met, this information is not relevant at all. So, exactly how is it that "it works there, there, and there" is supposed to provide evidence that it will work here?

That's the rub. The argument could be by enumerative induction: swan 1 is white, swan 2 is white . . .; so all swans are white—x plays a causal role in situation 1, x plays a causal role in situation 2 . . .; so x plays a causal role everywhere. How good is that argument? Induction demands a large and varied inductive base—lots of swans from lots of places; lots of RCTs from different populations. It also requires that the observations be generalizable, or "projectable," plus an account of the range across which they project. Electron charge is projectable everywhere—one good experiment can generalize to all; bird color sometimes is; causality is erratic—sometimes it generalizes and sometimes it does not. It cannot be relied on to generalize for well-known reasons. Causal connections often depend on intimate, complex interactions among factors present. No special role can be prized out and projected to new situations where these interactions do not occur.

Lots of positive RCT results are a good indicator that the policy plays the same causal role widely enough to reach to you. But you are always betting on a hidden premise: that the studies vary across enough different kinds of circumstances to generalize—and indeed across just the ones that matter for your situation. That bet is always a little dicey. And it is very difficult to have warrant for it when you are completely in the dark about what kinds of variation matter.

Alternatively, those who prefer more RCTs to horizontal and vertical search urge that, surely, the best evidence that the policy will work here is an ad hoc, local RCT here. We agree this could be good evidence. *Could be,* were it possible. It is not possible to do an RCT on the same population as the target, and at the same time as the proposed implementation. Both matter. We can sample, but a sample is almost never *representative*; that is, governed by the same causal principles and having the same probability distribution over causally relevant factors.

This has been an especially vexing problem in medical trials for a variety of reasons. First, trials must be done where they can actually be carried out—in hospitals that have the technology to administer the treatment under test, in locations where the staff is expert enough to monitor outcomes, and where large enough numbers of subjects are willing to participate. In addition, many types of subjects will be excluded for both scientific and ethical reasons. For instance, subjects taking other drugs may be excluded, since the pure effect of the treatment under test will not be observed if the treatment and the other drugs interact to produce special, nonstandard effects; these same subjects may also be excluded because they are not deemed healthy enough to enter the test. Those too old, too young, and unable to give informed consent may be excluded as well.

Time, too, cannot be ignored, especially when it comes to social policy. Are the causes the same now at the time you intend to implement the policy as they were when the study was done? That, as we have stressed, can be a serious worry. Populations change, social relations change, and in consequence so do the causal principles that determine what works. And recall from I.B.4, as Robert Lucas warns, that interventions can themselves change the very principles you are relying on to produce the effects that you predict. Of course, the experimental population could be representative enough and the causes stable enough. Let's just get this stated explicitly as one of the premises so that the need for warrant for it is transparent.

What you are after when you infer from a number of successes in other cases to success in your case, or success in general, is what is sometimes called "proof of concept." You want to know that if you do this in a wide variety of contexts that are by some test or other appropriate, it will work. That, we maintain, is best done by thinking about causal roles and support factors. And though this involves effort, can be difficult, and will never be done well enough that you can afford not to hedge your bets, it is not something that is at all beyond ordinary policy makers and policy analysts. It is what you do regularly when you deliberate seriously, even if you do not think of it that way.

IV.B.4 THINKING ABOUT CAUSAL ROLES AND SUPPORT FACTORS: THE RESTAURANT ROLL OUT

Here is an example of how you find out why what you did worked or failed, and how you have to use or try to establish generalizations as background (not at first unconscious) knowledge to decide to do more.

Take a business that has opened five restaurants in the last year.[2] Of these, one has not worked. It will never make the money it should but is kept open because it generates cash. Three are more or less as planned—good sales, well-controlled costs, and decent profits. One is very successful. So overall, the company is doing well. And so there is some evidence that it worked there; and that it didn't work there. We haven't got proof of concept, confidence that if we open more, enough will work. Because we don't know enough about how it works. In our language, we haven't got answers to questions about causal roles and support factors.

The decision now is whether to open 10 more of the same. But the doubters (usually the bankers) want more discussion. They need to be satisfied about questions like these:

1. Five is a small enough number for the senior, experienced managing director to have supervised very closely exactly how each was designed and fitted out to suit the nature of the building, how the launch and its publicity suited the expected market, and all the other small, but in the aggregate important, peculiarities of each site. She also worked 14 hours a day to make sure that everything worked. This can't be done for the next 10 by her or anyone else. That work will have to be delegated to her deputy who is good, but younger and less experienced.

2. Similarly, running the five requires a lot of detailed supervision by that deputy, a good deal of which is peculiar to the individual restaurant. If she is expected to open 10 new sites next year, she will have to delegate that work to the local restaurant managers, who are even younger and even less experienced, which is possibly why they have needed supervision.

3. We need to understand why the bad one failed and why the excellent one succeeded. If, of the next 10, only one is excellent, and two fail, we will be in trouble. We need to know what "the same" means. They are not literally the same—they are in different places for a start. What is the story behind why three worked, one flopped, and one was tremendous; that is, how did they work—what are the general features, like the ones discussed for CCTV in III.B.3.1, that allowed the successful ones to work?

4. What anyway is the evidence on which this decision to expand is based? What facts do you rely on?

The board room debate goes on.

1.1 Agreed. We know that pilots— and the five can be seen as a pilot— typically produce results that cannot be replicated, just because they have been intensely incubated in a way that cannot continue on a larger scale. But our experience, and the experience of others, shows that this effect is quite small in cases like ours. Our profit forecasts for the 10 are a little lower than for the successes among the five, just for this reason.

2.1 We can fix this. We are appointing an operations manager to take over the job of supervising the five, and the 10 as they open. And the restaurant managers need less supervision as they get more experienced, teething problems are solved, and so on. That is all in the figures.

3.1 We think that the following are the main factors that determined the degree of success of the five:

   3.1.1 The formula appeals to rather older and rather more conservative people than we expected. That is why Notting Hill failed—they want something more striking than good French food at a reasonable price. Market towns are better than cities.

   3.1.2 Obviously, but we underestimated it, the competition matters. We do well where there are few or no middling to good Italian, Spanish, or French restaurants.

   3.1.3 All the five do well for special events—birthdays, office parties, Christmas. But not everywhere has people who just go out to eat because they fancy it, don't want to cook, like a treat. That is why we won't go to Edinburgh. Scots don't go out in the evening so much.

All these questions are the questions you ask if you are trying to establish what a policy needs in order to work. They are questions of the kind that we recommend generally when you are deciding "Will it work here?" Of course, in thinking about a particular new location, you take into account that it worked (or didn't work) there. But that is not because such experience gives you a conclusion about here. What it does, as the above process shows, is prompt more or less helpful thoughts about why it worked, and those questions are our questions.

In the case of the Greater London Authority, discussed below, the question is "If it worked there in Seattle, will it work here in London?" We say that to answer that, you have to think about how it worked in Seattle. And when you have done that, and you cannot expect a wholly certain set of answers, try it out in London. Just as if the engineers tell you that it will fly, you must certainly see if it does. And despite our doubts expressed above about ad hoc local RCTs, trying it out will very likely be helpful, whether by RCT or otherwise. But not, for the reasons we gave, because it proves that it will work in Hackney. Rather, it will help you, as you try it out, to see better how it works here. The local RCT is only another example of "it worked there, then." The difference between our approach and the RCT approach is clarified by seeing what you get out of failure. In the case of just an RCT, a pure RCT, nothing, because you are not thinking about how or why, just whether, it works. But for us, failure makes us look harder to see why. It helps us.

In the case of the restaurants, it is obvious that you have to think, because you have no alternative. There is no temptation to do a local RCT or other trial—you can't try out a restaurant in Hackney without setting up a restaurant in Hackney, which is what you are trying to decide about.

The more you think like that, and the more restaurants you open that take account of your latest thinking about the answers to these questions, the better your answers become. In the end, like Pizza Express, you have opened so many and have thought about it so much, that you have proved the concept. You know that it will work there because it will play the requisite causal role there, and the conditions for it to operate will be met.

Then you can start to neglect the answers to these questions. You can make the selection of sites and the specification of the restaurant offer routine, formulaic. You can give the job to someone who has not had to think through the answers to our questions, who maybe wouldn't understand if she did. The question "It worked there, will it work here?" has become uninteresting. Of course the VW will start.

An anecdote by Gary Klein in *Sources of Power* (1999: 39–44) illustrates this. There is a potentially fatal condition to which premature babies are prone that can be treated successfully by antibiotics, provided it is diagnosed in time to allow a five-day course of treatment. Standard diagnostic methods, such as blood tests, can detect the condition, but typically only three days before it will cause death. The antibiotics do not have time to work. An experienced staff nurse in Boston General Hospital has a good track record of looking at babies and saying, without any tests, that they have the condition. She can do this early enough for the antibiotic course to work. Less experienced staff can't do this.

So the hospital tries to find out how the staff nurse does it. She doesn't know—she thinks that she just looks and decides. But with great difficulty she is able to surface what she is looking for—a combination of changed color, and heightened activity, and poor appetite. Some of these she does indeed get from just looking, some she gets from the hour-by-hour medical records, though she reads those routinely, without focusing on their relevance to this task.

With care, a list of such diagnostic points is drawn up and used to train the other nurses. The list is not infallible. But it helps the others to do the same as the staff nurse, by following the rules. After a bit, the other nurses know what to do, and don't have to look at the rules. Later, they can't remember the rules. They just say, as the staff nurse did at the beginning, that they look and see.

To start with, the problem—how to diagnose outside five days to death—was novel. You needed an experienced expert—the staff nurse—to deliberate about what facts were relevant and how you might establish them—by looking at the baby, reading the records. To start with, she did that unconsciously, though it was deliberation, nonetheless. Had she explored the problem openly with one of her colleagues, it would have been just like the board thinking about the restaurant expansion—what's going on, what facts matter.

This case study illustrates again the supreme importance of answering our questions. Certainly, you had to start by seeing whether there is something to be explained. Was the experienced nurse's success real? Did she beat chance? An RCT, or some other test of her performance against, for example, another nurse, will answer that. But then the hard work begins. You have to know not that she can do it, but how she does it. Without that, you cannot generalize her skill.

It also shows how our questions have to be answered, but that the answers can later slip into the background and be forgotten. When we say that we just know that penicillin fights infection, we forget because we know we can neglect how it works, just as we can neglect how the VW works. And if you evaluate the restaurant strategy by doing an RCT (forget the problems) it will get a good result. And the person who knows absolutely nothing about restaurants, call her the investor, can then see that restaurants like that make money. She does not have to understand the answers to our questions. But you would never have got to being able to neglect them if they had not been answered. We only got to being able to treat opening restaurants as though we were operating a machine because somebody answered the questions.

Note that our concern about RCTs is not about practicalities. Of course, in the restaurant case, and certainly in many social policy cases, you can't do RCTs. But even if possible morally or practically, they do not take you very far. That it worked there for some reason is a starting point for answering our questions. But only a starting point. To be confident that the policy will work here you need to know that it can play a positive causal role here and that you have the support factors necessary for it to do so.

IV.B.5 WHAT'S LEFT FOR RCTs

To summarize, for reliable effectiveness predictions, a solid starting point—which a good RCT can deliver—is a good start. But only a start, one stone on the long, and often tortuous, road to "it will work here." And it is neither the only nor always the best start. Figure IV.1 provides a graphic image of

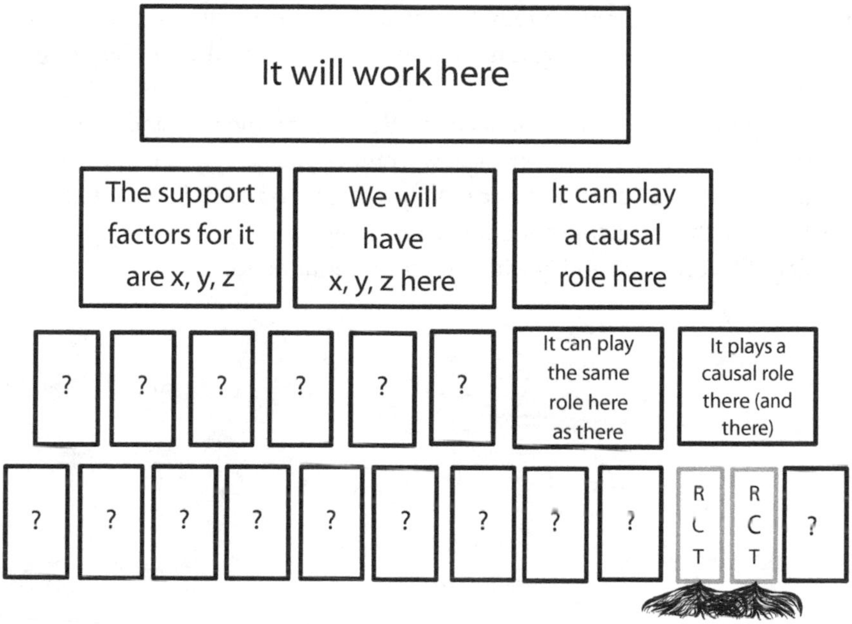

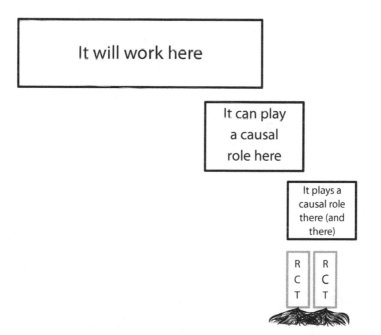

Figure IV.1: The argument pyramid for effectiveness predictions

Figure IV.2: Effectiveness prediction with only RCT support

what it takes to warrant a prediction that the policy will make a positive contribution in your setting. It is what, in I.B.2.1.a, we called an "argument pyramid."

To support the top row, you need to fill in the middle row, and do so in a sensible way with as much empirical warrant as you can garner. That's what horizontal and vertical searches can help with. If you can't fill in the rest of the boxes with reasonable confidence (as in figure IV.2), even superb RCT results will leave your policy with very flimsy foundations.

CHAPTER IV.C

✧

Evidence-Ranking Schemes, Advice Guides, and Choosing Effective Policies

E vidence-based policy is a good thing. Everyone would support the principle that a policy should be confronted with the facts before you bet that it will be effective. At such a high level of abstraction, that is uncontroversial. But, as we say in our account of the vertical ladder of abstraction, you have to be careful when you come to turn such high-level principles into operational policies that will work on the ground. The (still quite high-level) principle that we developed in our theory chapter was this: to know or bet that a policy will be effective here you need to know two key facts—that the policy can play a positive causal role here and that the support factors for it to operate are fulfilled here. That is a lower level (i.e., less abstract) principle than that a policy should be confronted with the facts. It is still not low-level enough to be fully operational—it does not tell you what are the specific facts that you have to establish if you are to adopt this policy here. But it is precise enough to allow us to compare it with what you are meant to do if you follow the advice that often seems to be suggested in the evidence-based policy literature. And that is what we now set out to do, by first giving an account of what that literature says.

We must be clear what the status of this account is. It is not a comprehensive survey of the literature. We have not read it all. And the schema that we use for our discussion is not meant to represent any particular, or the average, or the typical, or the representative, member of the literature. It is intended to pick out features of the literature that are found widely, and therefore enable us to contrast what they say with what we say. So if you look at any particular evidence-based policy paper, you may not find all the features that we have in our schema, and you are very unlikely to find them in the same form as we present them.

This is our schema. We distinguish:

1. Evidence-ranking schemes. These say, for example, that the best evidence for a policy is a systematic review or a meta-analysis of well-conducted RCTs. And they go on to list other types of evidence in descending order. This does not of itself tell you what to do.
2. Advice guides. These say, for example, that you should choose a policy that is backed by good evidence, using the ranking in the schemes. This does not tell you which policies these are.
3. Warehouses. This is where you find policies backed by good evidence. The managers of the warehouse have only put onto the shelves policies that have met that test.

It could be—and the Department of Education's *User Friendly Guide*[1] seems an example here—that at least the first two stages are conflated. RCTs are best and choose a policy backed by RCTs. Similarly, it may be that the Campbell Collaboration[2] conflates all three: on our shelves there are policies approved by us that you should choose because they are based on good RCT evidence. But the schema is not here to help classify the literature. It is intended to do no more than disentangle the various functions that in one way or another the evidence-based policy literature appears to fulfill, and to help compare it with what we say.

What, then, is the literature like? Here is a non-comprehensive list of sites that aim to help with judging policy effectiveness in various areas or that vet and warehouse policies:

- SIGN: Scottish Intercollegiate Guidelines Network
- GRADE: Grading of Recommendations Assessment, Development and Evaluation
- What Works Clearing House
- USEPA: US Environmental Protection Agency
- CEPA: Canadian Environmental Protection Act
- Cochrane Collaboration
- Campbell Collaboration
- California Evidence-Based Clearinghouse for Child Welfare
- Substance Abuse and Mental Health Services Administration's National Registry of Evidence-based Programs and Practices
- Oxford Centre for Evidence-Based Medicine
- National Institute of Justice: Preventing Crime: *What Works, What Doesn't, What's Promising*

We say that:

1. Evidence-based policy as it is operated, or meant to operate, at present is dominated by schemes and guides and warehouses of the kind exemplified in this list.
2. The central tendency of such literature is to rank RCTs, or meta-analyses, or systematic reviews of RCTs, as gold standard evidence for effectiveness, and urge that, if at all possible, policy makers choose only policies backed by such evidence, and look for them in approved warehouses.

The weasel word "tendency" recognizes that not many, maybe none, will do that fully and explicitly. It may not be insisted on, maybe just recommended as generally the best bet. There may not be a warehouse yet for your policy area. And so on.

But our concern is that the bulk of the literature presently recommended for policy decisions in the United States and the United Kingdom cannot be used to identify "what works here." And this is not because it may fail to deliver in some particular cases—any procedure can, or will, fail sometimes. It is not that its advice fails to deliver what it can be expected to deliver—the rules are actually good at identifying policies that work, that is, *policies that work somewhere*. The failing is rather that it is not designed to deliver the bulk of the key facts required to conclude that it will work here.

Figure IV.3 pictures a particularly reflective scheme for ranking evidence. GRADE was constructed by the Grading of Recommendations Assessment, Development and Evaluation Working Group and is used by over 50 organizations worldwide (Balshem et al. 2011: 404).

Table IV.1 provides GRADE's 2011 definitions of what the different evidence ranks mean.

Study design	Initial quality of a body of evidence		Lower if	Higher if	Quality of a body of evidence
Randomized trials	High ⟶		Risk of bias -1 Serious -2 Very serious	Large effect +1 Large +2 Very large	High (four plus: ⊕ ⊕ ⊕ ⊕)
			Inconsistency -1 Serious -2 Very serious	Dose response +1 Evidence of a gradient	Moderate (three plus: ⊕ ⊕ ⊕ ○)
Observational studies	Low ⟶		Indirectness -1 Serious -2 Very serious	All plausible residual confounding +1 Would reduce a demonstrated effect	Low (two plus: ⊕ ⊕ ○ ○)
			Imprecision -1 Serious -2 Very serious	+1 Would suggest a spurious effect if no effect was observed	Very low (one plus: ⊕ ○ ○ ○)
			Publication bias -1 Likely -2 Very likely		

Figure IV.3: A summary of GRADE's approach to rating quality of evidence. From Balshem et al. 2011: 404.

Table IV.1. SIGNIFICANCE OF THE FOUR LEVELS OF EVIDENCE

Quality level	Definition
High	We are very confident that the true effect lies close to that of the estimate of the effect
Moderate	We are moderately confident in the effect estimate: The true effect is likely to be close to the estimate of the effect, but there is a possibility that it is substantially different
Low	Our confidence in the effect estimate is limited: The true effect may be substantially different from the estimate of the effect
Very low	We have very little confidence in the effect estimate: The true effect is likely to be substantially different from the estimate of the effect

Source: From Balshem et al. 2011: 404.

There are many things to be said about the detail of this or any other similar ranking, and why some lists include somewhat different phraseology and rankings. We noted some oddities with it in I.B.5.3, but our real concern is not with that sort of detail. We are happy to accept that GRADE provides a conscientious and intelligent ranking of what study designs produce good evidence. Our concern is rather to be clear what good evidence, say "high quality" evidence, is evidence *for*. You need it to be evidence for the effectiveness of a policy. And by effectiveness, like everyone else, we mean that it will work in the context where it will be applied ("here").

So how much do these schemes contribute to establishing that the policy will work here? Just what can their "high quality" evidence establish? As we discussed in IV.B, ideal studies of the kinds demanded for this ranking clinch the fact that the policy played a positive causal role somewhere, and perhaps in many somewheres. We agree that that is a considerable achievement. And we agree with the lists that the other less highly ranked sources of evidence are worse at that than are RCTs, except in cases where very specific background causal information can be added. And we agree with GRADE's assessment that expert opinion is bad at providing evidence that the policy played a positive causal role anywhere, let alone at clinching it. So our quarrel is not with the rankings but with how far their top ranked evidence can take you in predicting that your policy will work here.

RCTS clinch the fact that the policy played a positive causal role in the study population. But they do little to establish the fact that the policy can play the same, or any, positive causal role here and even less to establish that the necessary support factors will be present. Those are not the facts that they are in the business of clinching.

The importance of RCTs in our argument pyramid was illustrated in figure IV.1 from IV.B. In the bottom right corner is the "it plays a positive causal role there (and there)" box. Below it are two RCT boxes, which represent one way, but only one way, of establishing that it works somewhere. And the rest of the boxes have question marks, because RCTs say nothing about them.

In terms of our distinction between trustworthiness and relevance, to take results graded "high quality" by the ranking schemes as good enough evidence that the policy will work in your setting is to make a bad presupposition about relevance: that the only facts seriously relevant to predicting that a policy will work for you is that the policy worked somewhere. The evidence that is ranked "high quality" is only indirectly relevant for you. It can support "it works here," but it does so via the support that it offers for "it works somewhere." And whether it is evidence at all is conditional on the other boxes being filled in reasonably well.

Because relevance matters, and everyone knows that it does, the guides will generally make an effort to draw your attention to this. For instance, the US Department of Education's *User Friendly Guide* from 2003, as well as their more up-to-date Web advice, says that strong evidence for your policy is two or more high quality RCTs. So far, so familiar. But it also says that these RCTs should be carried out in "school settings similar to yours" and, as an example to clarify, that trials in white suburban populations do not constitute strong evidence for large inner-city schools serving primarily minority students. Of course they don't. The rankings that the Department of Education focuses on are concerned with quality—quality of evidence that the policy worked somewhere. The reference to white suburban schools is a reference to relevance. And that we think needs a book and some theory, not a sentence.

What has gone wrong? Go back to what we said in III.B. We all agree—the authors of the guides, the authors of this book, everyone—with the principle that policy should be confronted with the facts. We all surely agree that we need to tease out what we mean by the facts; and the addition of the word "relevant" cannot be controversial. But no sooner added, that word cries out for an answer to the question, "What makes a fact relevant?" And at that point, we say, you are stuck with having to have an account of how the policy is going to work if it does work. "A Land Rover can negotiate this rough terrain, and it needs fuel." Both these propositions have to be true, and there has to be fuel.

We now look in greater detail at three recent examples of evidence-based policy that we applaud because they take on issues of relevance. The first is the remarkably comprehensive and scholarly 2011 report by

UK Member of Parliament Graham Allen, *Early Intervention: The Next Steps* (Allen 2011), which includes a list of 72 programs that fulfill the criterion of cost effectiveness, with 19 in the top category, Level 1. To be Level 1, a program has to pass[3] the following tests (ibid. 119, 135, and 137):

1. Be supported by one RCT or two quasi-experimental designs.
2. Have a positive impact on an Allen-desired outcome. It must contribute to the aims of early intervention.
3. Have no iatrogenic effect. The intervention must not produce undesired side effects.
4. There are no obvious concerns about intervention specificity or system readiness. The success of the policy must not be obviously local or special. And, for example, the resources needed must be available where you are intending to apply the policy.
5. The risk and promotive factors that the intervention seeks to change are identified, using the intervention's logic model or theory explaining why the intervention may lead to better outcomes.
6. Meet a "best" criterion on evaluation quality or impact.
7. Do the results indicate the extent to which fidelity of implementation affects the impact?
8. Do the results hold up for different age groups, boys and girls, ethnic minority groups?
9. Is there is verification of the theoretical rationale underpinning the intervention, provided by mediator analysis showing the effects are taking place for the reasons expected?

Allen's work certainly, like the bulk of the evidence-based policy literature, headlines the importance of RCTs. This is the gateway that any policy has to get through if it is to be Level 1. But that is only test one in his list. And many of his other eight tests, for example, 9 above, reflect concern with the kind of issues, issues of relevance, that preoccupy us.

The Greater London Authority (GLA 2010: 14) also recognizes explicitly that what worked there may not work here, as you see in box IV.1.

And as we have seen above Allen goes even further:

> There is verification of the theoretical rationale underpinning the intervention, provided by mediator analysis showing the effects are taking place for the reasons expected. (2011: 135, A13)

And elsewhere:

Box IV.1

THE CULTURAL COMPETENCE BOX

London is one of the most diverse cities in the world. Programmes that are designed in one part of London may seem less appealing to another. Many models achieving high marks on the Standards come from places far away including the United States, Norway, Ireland, Australia and Tanzania.

An obvious question is 'how do we know if a policy or programme proven to work in, for example, Seattle, will work in London?' Or, possibly, 'how do we know if an intervention meeting the Standards in, for example, Richmond will work in Hackney?'

The simple answer is 'if in doubt, evaluate and find out'. To take a practical example, the Incredible Years parenting programme, that originated in Washington State on the West Coast of the US, has been re-tested in Ireland, Wales, Birmingham and South London. Are these results sufficient for a commissioner in, for instance, Islington? Only local commissioners can make that judgement. They may decide there is sufficient evidence, or they may decide to evaluate the programme in a randomised controlled trial to make sure results stand up.

There is by now a strong literature concerning the cultural competence of evidence based policies and programmes. The core elements of proven interventions, aimed at reducing risks to children's health and development, tend to apply equally well to many ethnic groups. Indeed, a good test of the robustness of an evidence-based programme is the extent to which it continues to work effectively in different cultural contexts.

Source: GLA 2010: 14.

The risk and promotive factors that the intervention seeks to change are identified, using the intervention's logic model or theory explaining why the intervention may lead to better outcomes. (Ibid. 137, C3)

Finally, the American Psychological Association's "Criteria for Evaluating Treatment Guidelines" (APA 2002:1056–57) deals extensively with relevance as well. For example:

Criterion 6.0: Guidelines should reflect the breadth of patient variables that may affect the clinical utility of the intervention.

Criterion 8.0: It is recommended that guidelines take into account information pertaining to the setting in which the treatment is offered.

These—and there are others—recognize the importance of relevance and begin to confront it. The GLA in particular provides strategies to help discover what may be relevant to the effectiveness of a policy. For instance, it recommends that you:

> do not change the core elements of an evidence based programme without good evidence that changes are needed. Second, work hard to ensure that the surface elements of programmes and policies intended to improve child outcomes are sensitive to the community's characteristics and desires. . . . Third, when adapting an existing proven model check back with the programme originator and other commissioners or providers of the intervention to get advice about adaptation. (2010: 14)

What do we make of these efforts? We agree with much of their advice. But it is unsystematic. It sounds like a conversation one has entered midstream. Yes, the suggestions make sense. But what kind of theory backs them up? And are these the only considerations? Or the most important? Are there other very different kinds of considerations that matter? And how can you know what matters? That's the question we tackle. What matters, we say, is information that helps you tell what causal role the policy can play in your setting and what support factors would allow it to do so. We provide a general framework for marshalling the information you need. And you can believe in this framework because it is grounded in a reliable theory, a theory about the nature of evidence and about how causes work to produce their effects. We all admire the framework within which RCTs warrant trustworthiness. We want to provide a framework for talking about relevance.

Look again at the GLA, in more detail. The GLA says not to change the core elements unless you have evidence that changes are needed. When is that? You are also told to check back with the program originators before making these changes. The program originators face the same question you do. When are changes to the core elements needed? Changes are needed when—and only when—the original core elements cannot play the same causal role in the new community as in the communities where the program worked before. Similarly, the surface elements referred to by the GLA are merely a symptom of what matters. You need to ensure that the new community has all the support factors necessary for the program to play its positive causal role or the program won't work in the new community.

The final GLA tip is: "Ultimately a balance must be found between being culturally sensitive and not compromising the fidelity of intervention delivery" (2010: 14). It is hard to see how to make this general advice operational without enquiring how the intervention works and why it might not work. That requires having a theory of causal roles and support factors, and techniques, like those in III, for identifying what these are for your policy in your setting. Sometimes it will be right to put the program into effect unchanged. Sometimes it will need major modification. Which of these is true for you depends on what's true about causal roles and support factors. It is not a matter of balance.

It is also suggested that if there is insufficient evidence that a policy that worked there will work here, it may be necessary "to evaluate the programme in a randomised controlled trial to make sure results stand up" (ibid.). There is plenty of experience to show that it is very hard in the policy arena to carry out RCTs that can lead to being at all sure. The standard problems—dilution effects, neighborhood effects, selection bias for entry into the study, the difficulty of getting large enough samples in a small population—are all major obstacles. And given the typical time lag—because of the politics, the money, public opinion—between a successful test, if you get one, and implementation, there is always the danger that things will have changed in your target population or otherwise when you come to intervene. We do not think that even local RCTs can substitute for understanding how the policy is meant to work.

There are similar problems with Allen. He produces a list of Level 1 programs that have had to pass tests that include, among other considerations, the relevance criteria listed above. But once the list has been promulgated, there is nothing to tell the users, the policy makers who want to bet on, for example, Surestart, whether it will work for them. To get on the list, Surestart had to have worked in accordance with "the reasons expected." But how do you know whether those are the reasons that you would expect to make it work here? Lists like the Allen list do not provide them. This is what our framework is designed to help you do.

CHAPTER IV.D

⟟

Fidelity

Sometimes when a policy has been shown by good studies to have worked somewhere, or better, in a number of somewheres, you are enjoined to implement the policy exactly as it was done in the study situations. This is the principle of *fidelity*.

As we have just seen, the current Greater London Authority guidelines (GLA 2010) for the adoption of social policies in London emphasize that if you are to use an intervention that worked somewhere else, you should execute it exactly as it was executed where it was successful.[1] Some commercial suppliers of reading and other policy packages insist that the package be implemented exactly as the supplier says. You can see why. They cannot be responsible for failure if the instructions aren't followed. The cake won't rise if you don't follow the recipe.[2]

There will be cases where the postmortem does indeed finger infidelity as the problem.[3] The mistake in California was to think that the truth of the proposition that it worked in Tennessee was by itself very good evidence that it would work for you. What went wrong was that there weren't enough good teachers, and not enough classrooms, whereas in Tennessee they got both of those right. So a faithful execution of the policy as it was executed in Tennessee would indeed have worked, and infidelity was the problem. In our terms, you needed to be faithful to what the cake said, and then all would have been well.

The policy in Britain of culling badgers to reduce bovine TB was based in part on the conclusions of the Randomized Badger Culling Trial (RBCT), which showed that proactive badger culling resulted in an overall beneficial effect compared with "no cull" areas (Bourne et al. 2007). But scientists expert in this field warned[4] that the more that a future culling policy deviates from the conditions of the RBCT—industry versus government led and/or differences in culling methods (such as permitted controlled shooting of badgers in addition to cage-trapping), the more likely it is that the effects of that policy will differ, either positively or negatively. And the policy as proposed did indeed differ in its culling methods from those tested in the RBCT.

Our theoretical framework helps to sort out the issues that arise from fidelity. We say that for the policy to work, it has to play a positive causal role here and that the support factors for it to operate have to be fulfilled here. The advice "be faithful" must then presuppose that the policy plays the same causal role here as there, that the program builds in support factors that will be equally necessary in both places, and that any additional support factors necessary in your situation that are not built into the program can be expected to obtain. If you have good reasons for believing all of that, then of course it is very good advice to be faithful. Otherwise, by monkeying around with the program, you may delete necessary support factors or change the causal role the program can play. You can even turn a beneficial program into a monster.

The admonition by the scientists to stick closely to culling methods shown to work by the RBCT is suitably unspecific. It says that if you are not faithful, who knows what will happen. And we agree with that. We even agree that if you are right (though how do you know it?) to assume that the policy will play the same causal role here and that the support factors will be present, fidelity will get you the result. But we say that assumption is much too strong to take as a default position, one you can rely on unless you have reason to the contrary.[5] So you cannot avoid our question, "What are the facts that are relevant to this intervention?"

The BINP example shows that fidelity may well not be the best idea. Even if in Bangladesh they did exactly what was done in Tamil Nadu, they went wrong because those were not the relevant facts. The cake that worked in Tamil Nadu did not work in Bangladesh. You had to go up and down the ladder of abstraction to see what the relevant cake was.

It is true, as we say in IV.B, that if you find many examples of an intervention working there, you have a good start on warranting the claim that it works widely and maybe even widely enough to cover your situation. But if it has worked often in exactly the same circumstances that is not very helpful at showing it works widely. It is like reading the same newspaper twice. The replication that is taken as an important test of the validity of a specific RCT is desirable precisely because it seeks to confirm that you get the result when for the second and the third . . . time you replicate the result in the same circumstances, with the same things held constant. That is a standard test of replicability in science—can someone else get the same result in the same circumstances? If you can't, that makes the original result suspect for having arisen from some misstep in the experiment or from a statistical anomaly—after all, every once in a long while you should expect 10 heads in a row from flipping a fair coin. This is one good reason for the US Department of Education to suggest using policies that have *two* good RCTs in their favor.[6]

As we say in the Fight for Peace case study we describe below, you could say that it all depends on what you mean by saying that the intervention has worked often in the same circumstances. If that means literally in the *same* circumstances (but what could that mean?), then we have replication without any hints about generalizability. But if it has succeeded often in circumstances that differ greatly, then multiple successes are very helpful. They suggest strongly that the policy plays a positive causal role across a variety of different circumstances, and it may well be that your circumstances are a member of that class of circumstances.

If the appeal for fidelity is not "do exactly the same thing in exactly the same way," but that you do something that is faithful to the higher level principle that was instantiated by the previous success, then that is fine. But you have then to do a lot of work to see what you actually do in your case—to climb down the ladder of abstraction—and it will be a special case if it is the same as in the previous situation where just that proved effective.

All this matters because circumstances do vary. Consider what a group of well-known experts argue about drug policy:

> There is no single drug problem within or across societies; neither is there a magic bullet that will solve "the" drug problem. Societies differ substantially in the specific drugs that are problematic, the patterns in which drugs are used, the damage associated with drug distribution and use, and the ways in which various substances are controlled, among myriad other factors. There are significant variations as well within societies, for example between the sexes, across races, and age groups, at different stages of a drug epidemic. There is as a result no single globally homogeneous "drug problem." It follows from this realization that there can be no single or universal solution to the drug problem, either within a society or across societies. The desire for a "magic bullet" be it a new program of servicers, a change in the legal regime, or the concentration of resources into a "war on drugs" is understandable. However, to quote H. L. Mencken, "[f]or every complex question, there is an answer that is clear, simple and wrong." We offer this caution about the search for a simple solution to a complex drug problem, including the assumption that the same drug policy will have the same impact on different societies. (Babor et al. 2010: 253)

It is very unlikely that even quite a few successful experiences of "it worked there" will provide a very good drug program that can play a positive causal role almost everywhere.

We now provide two examples to illustrate the importance of not following to the letter what has worked there.

Fight for Peace[7] (FFP) uses boxing and martial arts combined with education and personal development to realize the potential of young people in communities that suffer from crime and violence. It has a clear set of familiar, high-level aims (Madgin 2008: 1):

- Prevent youth crime
- Reintegrate youth back into society
- Reduce poverty of opportunity
- Foster social inclusion

The program identifies six risk factors that make it hard to achieve these outcomes:

- Poverty/inequality of wealth
- Lack of economic options
- Social marginalization
- Violence
- Family groups
- Lack of leisure facilities/boredom

To deal with these obstacles there are five so-called "pillars" designed to alter the decision-making processes of young people to give knowledge, confidence, and self-esteem to avoid the risk factors. Here are the five pillars:

- Boxing and martial arts
- Personal development
- Social actions
- Access to labor markets
- Youth leadership

These aims, the risk factors, and the five pillars are common to both Rio and London. But what differs is how the five pillars are put into practice in the two locations.

In London, the following activities are undertaken for each pillar (Sampson 2009: 4):

- Boxing and martial arts: professional trainers are used and young people are entered for competitions
- Personal development: includes sessions on drugs, sexual health, gangs, and crime

- Social action: includes outreach work, contact with parents/carers, meetings with local residents and other community groups
- Access to labor markets: includes literacy and numeracy work, job application and interviewing skills, careers advice, and work placements
- Youth leadership: youth councils, leadership courses, and being FFP ambassadors at public meetings

There are, of course, levels of detail, rungs of the ladder of abstraction, even lower than this. What exactly is meant, operationally, by contact with parents is not self-evident from the phrase itself. But this is how it works in East London, at this level of abstraction. Before we talk about fidelity, it is worth looking at this account of what they do and why, and seeing how it fits with our theory.

First, there is great deal of climbing up and down the ladder. The six risk factors are fairly high level. The notion of "lack of economic opportunity" has to be turned into something concrete, specific to these young people in East London, if you are to move down via "access to labor markets" to the list of particular interventions (literacy and numeracy work, etc.) that in London helps to achieve the high-level objectives you first thought of— for example, reduce poverty of opportunity. So this account of how Fight for Peace sets about its mission maps well onto our notion of the ladder of abstraction.

Second, at the lowest level of abstraction, where you are talking about what you do on the ground, what particular interventions you are going to put into effect, our account comes into play. There are causal roles. If the outcome is to reduce street violence, then channeling aggression into boxing and martial arts will contribute. There are also support factors—it is no good having boxing classes unless they are taught by serious professionals and they have some purpose—for instance, to get entered for a competition. That is what we call having all the ingredients in the cake.

Third, one of the attractive features of FFP for us is that it is heavily research-and evidence-based, is successful in both Rio and East London, and uses no evidence of the kind privileged by the ranking schemes.

The notion of fidelity comes into it like this. Fight for Peace started in Rio. It worked. Youth crime went down among the young people who took part in the program. So it looked a good idea to have a Fight for Peace program in London, which faced much the same problem. At the highest level of the ladder, there is the same list of familiar, high-level aims. So you could say that it was the same problem, and so you should apply the same interventions. And Fight for Peace does indeed think that what you should do is the same at the level of the five pillars.

But to see what that means at the lower, operational level in London, considerable time and effort was devoted to finding out how you deliver the five pillars there. That work certainly included sending London staff to Rio to see how it worked there. But it also required a prolonged consultation process in London with young people to identify what would affect the practice and the formation of Fight for Peace in London (Madgin 2008: 2).

The five pillar model is the model that is replicated across countries. But what you actually do in each country will differ, and little general can be said about how it will be different. It would be completely unsurprising if, say, family structures in the favelas were quite different from those in the East End of London, and if consequently what is meant by contact with parents is quite different.

A graphic example is how you recruit members to come to the clubs. In Rio, unimaginably to a Londoner, you can approach drug gang leaders to see which of their workers might be suitable. In Rio, the drug trade is much more straightforwardly a source of teenage employment. It is recognized that young boys may want to leave the trade and do something else. The leaders do not stand in their way. So asking them for suggestions is perfectly workable. It is hard to envisage that in London, or Baltimore as depicted in *The Wire*. So in London a main source was the supervisors of the FOCUS hostel in E14.[8] Another example is that in London, homelessness is an issue for the intervention. In Rio it is not, because there is no government housing for the homeless, so tapping into that was not part of the intervention in Rio.[9] Then again, in Rio a classroom setting is respected and enjoyed. In London, it is rejected because it is like school, so you have to use a gym and much less formal sessions than traditional lessons (Madgin 2008: 11).

And so on. Two things may be said about this, both we think wrong. First, the points are well made but trivial. They are not enough to derail the idea that it is a good bet just to do in London what you did in Rio. And we say that if you are lucky, very lucky, that may be true. If you don't think about such things, the world may be benign, and the number of differences like this may be few and in the aggregate harmless. It may even be that there are differences that make the intervention even more effective. But what we say is, why bet on it? The history of rollout failure is such that it is a bad bet.

Second, it will be said that taking things like that into account is just common sense. And it is true, as we illustrated with the restaurant example in IV.B, that how to think, deliberating on these things, is not a rarefied skill. Most people can do it, and do do it, when they are building a restaurant chain or launching a robot pen. In that sense the skill is common. But it is not common, or not common enough in policy making, to use that skill. Any policy making process that majors on "it worked there" and does not subject the decision to roll out to at least a prima facie commonsense test of whether the conditions are such that it will work here is relying on great optimism about the benignity of the world.

As the example of housing shows, it is possible for the intervention to work well even though a feature important in one place (London) is absent in the other (Rio). The requirement of fidelity is hard to fit with this. Does it mean that you have to ignore in London the availability of government housing? Does it mean, if Rio were to have to be faithful to London that you should not intervene because you are missing part of the package and so cannot be faithful? Or is fidelity to be read as "as faithful as possible"? But then you have to think what role the provision of housing plays. Is it essential—literally a necessary condition, an ingredient of the cake that must be there? Or can it be left out—in our terms, is there another cake that produces a positive contribution but does not contain this ingredient? But to proceed like that is not to conform with the fidelity principle, which tells you nothing about how to sort out what matters. It is, just as we say, to think.

Another feature of the process of deciding how to put FFP into practice in London is the emphasis on what they call "Theories of Change." They list the *Intended Mechanisms of Change* thus (Madgin 2008: 4–5):

1. *Boxing and Martial Arts*

Channel aggression, increase confidence, learn self-discipline, forces young people to think about the decisions they make through training and competitions.

2. *Education/Personal Development*

Group work, 1-2-1 conversations, role plays, imagery, DVDs, games to enable them to improve their decision-making process and understand the importance of making considered decisions which will help them inside and outside of school.

3. *Social Action: Promoting a Culture of Peace*

Methods of non-violent conflict resolution delivered through the boxing and martial arts activities and workshops to ensure young people do not turn to violence in order to solve their perceived problems. Increased opportunities for young people to access services as FFP staff evaluate the needs of young people and determine whether they need to be referred to an outside agency for educational, legal, medical and/or psychological assistance.

4. *Access to Labour Market*

Reduce the need for young people to turn to criminal activity to make a living, by having opportunities to access employment.

5. *Youth Leadership*

Give young people a sense of responsibility by making them the "voice" of the project.

This approach is an example of what we advocate in III.B.3: look for general features that can play the same causal roles broadly; then figure out what they amount to in the concrete in your situation. And it would be no surprise if the concrete list for London differed quite materially from that relevant to Rio.

Here is another example, this time of something that did not work (EFF 2005). Street (UK) was founded after the example of Poland's Fundusz Mikro and other international microfinance schemes. Fundusz Mikro had 15,000 clients using a group lending model and was financially self-sustaining after five years of operation. The modern-day pioneer of microcredit was Grameen Bank of Bangladesh, which was set up in the 1970s and has lent money to thousands of poor village entrepreneurs on a group lending basis. It seemed sensible, therefore, to use the same initiative to deal with the same kinds of problem in the United Kingdom. The problem, in general terms, is poor access to start-up money from traditional banks for small entrepreneurs. For instance;

> When Leigh and her daughter Yvonne needed funding to open their hairdressing salon in Handsworth, Birmingham they came up against a brick wall. The couple had identified a gap in the market in their neighborhood, where all the hairdressers specialized in Afro-Caribbean styles even though there was a significant white European population locally. "I was passed from pillar to post by both banks and other start-up organizations, who looked at our mother-daughter partnership and decided one of us was too old and the other one too young." (2005: 6)

In the proposal there was an account of the trends in the United Kingdom that were of concern (2005: 10):

1. The gap between the well paid employed and the low paid and unemployed.
2. The growing number of self-employed.
3. Reduced availability of trust-based appropriate business loans because of restructuring of the financial services industry.

So there was an outcome to be desired and an intervention that had worked. Accordingly, a charitable foundation provided support for the start-up, with £1.329m. It did not work. The number and quantum of loans were well below what had been planned and what could count as a major impact; they expected to help thousands of people rather than hundreds. What went wrong? It seems that the major difficulties were in the differences between the circumstances and character of the target market in Poland and the United Kingdom—and no doubt in Bangladesh, although that was not explicitly used as a comparator in either the proposal or the evaluation. What were those differences?

Group lending works like this. You form a group of, say, 10 possible borrowers. They meet and one of them puts up a proposal. The group evaluates it and if they agree a Community Development Finance Institution[10] (CDFI) or similar entity provides the money. The group, not the individual borrower, is responsible for meeting the interest and capital repayment obligations of the loan. So the group monitors the progress of the borrower's project, and it is the group that has to deal with defaults, late payments, and so on. This arrangement encourages honest assessment of projects and borrowers by one's peers. This is what is reported to have worked in Bangladesh and in Poland. Maybe because it is trust- and group-based, it turns out that women are often better at this than men. But it was hard to form such groups in the United Kingdom.

1. In other societies, particularly in the South, people trade and haggle over prices every day. Hence, there are more social linkages in the market place.
2. The target group in the United Kingdom is more diverse, and so it is hard to make up appropriately homogeneous groups.
3. Even poor people in the United Kingdom can get individual loans through credit cards. So maybe the need is just not there on a sufficient scale.
4. The tax and benefits system provides little incentive for people to graduate off welfare into self-employment because, typically, benefits terminate long before the business has generated sufficient income to manage without them.
5. Credit card and similar debt is available freely, without much or any scrutiny of creditworthiness of either the borrower or the project. A group or individual CDFI scheme requires the borrower to go through a rigorous assessment process. That is a deterrent even if it may be better for the client not to borrow, or not to borrow more than she can repay.
6. Regulatory and paperwork requirements generally are discouraging.

Finally, and very important, the board of Street (UK) was made up of people who knew about international microfinance but did not have any local experience. Any experience that might have varied enough to raise the possibility that local differences might be present and relevant would have been helpful. It may be that people with international, and therefore generic, experience, having seen how an uncritical read across from there to here can go wrong, will be good at raising the question, "What might be different here?" But more likely, they may just operate at the wrong level of what constitutes the same problem. They may think that to do the same in the United Kingdom means literally, at the low level of the detail of the implementation of the policy, do the same. They may do the equivalent of, in the Bangladesh nutrition program, giving the food to the mother. They do not reflect that you need to give it to the person who controls the food. This means the mother-in-law.

PART FIVE

Deliberation Is Not Second Best

CHAPTER V.A

Where We Are and Where We Are Going

The task of evidence-based policy and practice is to identify what evidence is needed to make good judgments about effectiveness. The current orthodoxy says that the best evidence is provided by RCTs and that other kinds of evidence are second best. This orthodoxy is set out in the evidence schemes, which give you rules for classifying the evidence available to you. They are about ranking. They rank evidence as good or bad according to how it has been obtained—by an RCT, good; from experience, bad.

Why should the fact that it worked in Tamil Nadu be evidence that it will work in Bangladesh? In IV we used our theory to show that the orthodoxy can lead you astray because it neglects relevance. And it does so because it does not pay attention to the entire argument necessary to get you from there to here. The kind of studies ranked in standard evidence schemes can be relevant to whether the policy will work here, since these kinds of studies can show that the policy played a positive causal role somewhere. But, as our theory explains, that only enters into an argument that it will work here if you have warrant for the additional premises: that the policy can play the same role here as there and that you will have the support factors necessary for it to do so in place post-implementation. The standard ranking schemes are thus woefully incomplete. They rank studies that can provide evidence for only one of the premises in the basic argument necessary to warrant an effectiveness prediction; and as we repeatedly warn: an argument is only as secure as its weakest premise.

We have hazarded that this problem will not have an easy fix. Mill's method of difference, which we described in I.B.5.1, provides a principled way to establish that a factor causes a specified result somewhere. As we noted, the bulk of evidence-ranking schemes assess designs according to how well they can ensure that the conditions for an ideal Mill's method-of-difference study are met. But for the other premises, there does not seem to be any single underlying scheme available, like the ideal method-of-difference design, that all studies that can support one of these premises aspire to. So there will be no easy way to rank how close they come to doing it well. So it is unlikely we will be able to produce evidence-ranking schemes for the other premises necessary to warrant the prediction that the policy will work here. That is one way in which the orthodoxy leads you astray.

This part of our book is about another way. This too can be seen as about second best. If a rule such as "follow the RCTs, and do so faithfully" were a good way of deciding about effectiveness, then certainly deliberation is second best (or worse), because it cannot be better than following the rules. And similarly, the ability to deliberate in order to use your discretion and judgment successfully in making effectiveness decisions would be irrelevant or worse.

To answer our central questions about causal roles and support factors, you have to think, to deliberate. Just as the orthodoxy has little to say about relevance, so it ignores deliberation, since deliberation is how you get to grips with relevance, and so, of course, if you ignore relevance, you ignore deliberation.

Here we show how the orthodoxy, which is a rules system, discourages decision makers from thinking about their problems, because the aim of rules is to reduce or eliminate the use of discretion and judgment, and deliberation requires discretion and judgment. The aim of reducing discretion comes from a lack of trust in the ability of operatives to exercise discretion well. Whether it is possible to reduce discretion depends on whether the process of deciding what will be effective, by answering our central questions, can be reduced to the operation of rules. We say that it often, or typically, cannot. And that if it cannot, the attempt to replace discretion with rules, such as "Do it if, or maybe only if, it has worked there," is very damaging. Deliberation is not second best, it is what you have to do, and it is not *faute de mieux* because there is no *mieux*.

Part V is also about what kind of people decision makers have to be if they are to deliberate well. In a rules-based world, such as that of the orthodoxy, the decision maker has scarcely anything to do, and so it scarcely matters what kind of person she is. She must have certain basic abilities, like being able to read, and be the kind of person who will conform. Just as the concept of entrepreneur in economics has little to do with being an entrepreneur, so the decision maker here has little to do with taking decisions, because the point of the rules is precisely to reduce discretion and the exercise of judgment. To deliberate in order to exercise discretion requires a rich list of intellectual and practical virtues that cannot be reduced to the virtue of conformity. Thus, the orthodoxy not only discourages deliberation, as unnecessary since the rules are superior, but selects in favor of operatives who cannot deliberate.

CHAPTER V.B

cℵɔ

Centralization and Discretion

V.B.1 GETTING STARTED

Policy decisions are only one member of a very large class. Making decisions is a regular part not only of official, political, and business life, but of normal life too. A great deal of what we say in this book about, for example, relevance is quite generic—it is hard to see how any decisions, or at least reflective decisions that result from deliberation, can avoid consideration of what facts are relevant and which of those are true. Consequently, we must remember that we are all experienced in making decisions, and, although policy decisions can often be difficult and complex, so can and are the decisions that all of us make, and make often, in our daily and professional lives.

Some analyses, which have come to be called Decision Making, such as game theory, rational choice theory, or economic rationality, are formal and even conclusive—if you formulate the problem like this, then the optimum decision is like that. But that kind of analysis is only one, narrow way of approaching a discussion of how to make decisions well. It describes a process that looks very different from much ordinary experience of deciding.

Our account is neither formal nor, in that sense, conclusive. It is much closer to how decisions are actually made. It will not provide the comfort of a rigorously structured process that will converge on an optimum result. We can provide a structured account of our theory, and, by the metaphors of horizontal and vertical search, give a principled analysis of INUS conditions and the role of higher level, more abstract, causal roles to illuminate that account. But when we come to recommendations about how to make decisions about effectiveness, we believe that, for social policy in particular, generally, or often, or certainly in the difficult cases that dominate policy discussions, you have to start by asking the policy maker to think. And that is by its nature a diffuse and unstructured process. It is not rules-based and systematic.

In saying that our process is closer to how decisions are actually made, we are not justifying our approach as being more real, or common sense, than Decision Making. It is perfectly possible that most real life decisions are just badly made. There is an optimum way of hitting a backhand in tennis, and that recommendation is not undermined by saying that is not the way most people do it. So much the worse for them.

We believe that our approach is better than more rigorous and structured processes. As soon as you focus on the notion of relevance, you are involved in an open-ended process that does not, on principle, admit of rules that tell you beyond reasonable doubt what is relevant. There are no clear criteria of relevance or stopping rules that tell you when you have cornered all that you need to think about.

We believe that if this is right, then a central problem with the use of RCTs, evidence-ranking schemes, and fidelity is that they attempt to impose structured, rules-based procedures, where success depends on the process we call thinking or deliberating, which cannot be replaced by such procedures. There is an analogy with contracts and trust. If you are going to work together with someone on a project that is complex, and that, because it extends into the future, will turn out to be complex in ways that you cannot work out ex ante, there is nevertheless a strong temptation to draw up a contract that sets out in advance how to deal with the decisions you will come across down the road. Faced with a decision in a year's time, go to the contract to see what to do. But, very often, it turns out that there cannot be a contract that successfully deals ex ante with all or even most eventualities. The partnership works well if you can trust the other person to deal with problems as they occur, in a sensible and cooperative fashion. If that trust is misplaced, then the arrangement will not work. But it wouldn't have worked if you had had a contract either. A contract is not typically a substitute for trust.

Similarly, with policy decisions it would be good to have a rule book that enables you to decide easily that to achieve this social goal, you should (say) adopt a policy that has worked elsewhere. But we say that such a rule book will not produce good results when what will work here is heavily dependent on the particular facts and factors that matter here; and you cannot decide what to do without thinking about what those may be and why they matter. If the thinking is wrong, then the policy will not work. But it wouldn't have worked if you had had rules either. Rules are not typically a substitute for thinking.

There are (at least) two reasons for wanting to impose a rules-based system. One is that highlighted by Gerd Gigerenzer.[1] Surely, it seems, if you want to forecast who will win tennis matches at Wimbledon, the more you know and the more expert you are, the better. You should think about what the courts are like, how long this competitor was off for injury last month, past results of meetings of these two, current rankings: the more you think, the better. That is the stuff of sports obsessive conversations in a thousand pubs (or *tavernas*, or bars, or . . .) every night. That is what we call deliberation (and incidentally, this is another example that shows that our notion of deliberation is nothing exotic, it goes on all the time). But what, Gigerenzer says, if it turns out that a good bet is to back Nadal just because he is the more famous player? And what if the results of that rule, called the recognition heuristic, are just as good as the results of thinking? Then it is better to impose that rule and ban thinking, for what might be called reasons of economy—you get the same result for less effort. And there are other heuristics that have the same property—they are quick and easy and at least as good as more elaborate procedures. We have already referred to one class of such heuristics in our discussion of quick exit trees in III.B.4.1.

This part of our book is not about the Gigerenzer-type cases. It is about the second reason for imposing a rule, that it is a good way for the center to delegate decisions to operatives on the ground. If it is for the state, or the municipality, or the school, or the hospital to put into effect policies for youth crime or child care or obesity, and if the center does not want them to decide for themselves, then there have to be rules imposed by the center to determine, or at least constrain, the agents. These rules may be legal in the full sense, or codes of conduct, or lists of best practice. They may be strict or leave some discretion. But our concern is first to discuss generally when the application of rules and the suppression of discretion works and when it doesn't, and then to see how that discussion illuminates our analysis of our particular concern here—the imposition of rules concerning what constitutes good evidence for effectiveness.

To anticipate, we conclude that the imposition of rules like "find a good RCT" is very likely to be harmful because, unlike in the Gigerenzer case or in the case of the manual for fixing a machine, it is likely to be hard to devise rules ex ante that substitute well for thinking; and that in that case the imposition of rules will be damaging.

V.B.2 RCTs AND EVIDENCE-RANKING SCHEMES AS A SET OF RULES

There are two limiting ways of making policy decisions, and indeed of making decisions generally. One is to reach for the rule book. It will tell you how to answer the question. You are left with very little discretion, and you don't have to exercise judgment. Just do what the manual says. The other extreme is to make up your own mind, using whatever deliberative techniques you decide are appropriate. Certainly, using your judgment and using your discretion will not be unstructured. Experience matters, and so do the facts. And you may even use some rules—either as approximations or rules of thumb, or because that bit of the problem (what a machine can be expected to do) can indeed be reduced to unequivocal propositions. But you are to be trusted to decide what is best overall, including what to do in those areas of the problem where there are no rules, or no good rules, or the rules obviously don't apply.

Between these extremes lie a wide variety of actual cases. If the operative has lots of freedom, as do general medical practitioners in Britain, then the recommendations of bodies such as the National Institute for Clinical Health and Excellence (NICE) are no more than guidance. If the rules are very tight—the US Department of Education says you must only use approved educational interventions if you want Title I funding—then the rules do bite. If these are the facts, the doctor has considerable discretion, the school board very little.

We do not have enough facts about how much bite the evidence rankings, and indeed evidence-based policy as currently advocated, have in the real world. As with all authoritarian systems, there is likely to be a big gap between what is published by the controlling central authority and what happens on the ground. But on the face of it, the prevalence of prescriptions such as those we have discussed in IV.C, by the Greater London Authority and by Graham Allen MP, points to a danger that many operatives now find themselves faced with rules that effectively restrict their freedom in ways that concern us. Specifically, the decision whether an intervention will be effective for them is likely to be narrowly constrained by the rule that evidence for effectiveness be limited to the evidence of an RCT that it worked there, and that there is, and should be, very little scope for the exercise of judgment and discretion, which in our language includes thinking.

It is true that, as we noted in IV.B.2, the US Department of Education, for example, nods in the direction of the exercise of judgment, and hence toward thinking, in the phrase "school settings similar to yours." But minor qualifications like that can at best suggest only that there may be a bit of fudging of the rules when it looks sensible. That is a long way from our central thesis—that in the analysis of what is needed to make decisions about effectiveness, the starting point is that you have to think about causal roles and support factors. And in practice a very common way of going wrong, with serious practical consequences in Bangladesh and in California, is to think that you should start with the rule and probably stick with it.

It is an important function of the guides that they are used in organizations, typically bureaucracies. Part of their appeal is that, like all rule books, they promise to help to make good decisions where a central problem is how to delegate what decisions to front line operatives. They appeal not just because they allegedly embody an infallible route to the truth, but because they can be handed over to operatives as a way to make the right decision without having to embark on the risky business of deciding on the ground what to do. They appear to offer a guaranteed answer to "What will work here?" They render unnecessary the deliberative techniques of horizontal and vertical search, and our Part III strategies, because no deliberation is needed.

V.B.3 A CASE STUDY

Our interest here is in disentangling what damage might be done, and how, by following rules that prevent thinking. We begin with a case study that starts by showing how good the use of rules can be at the early stage of a process, not just because they economize on the risks and costs of the alternative, but because they actually work better. Here is a nice example of how you follow the rules as far as you can, and then have to change to using your judgment (and in this case back again to following rules, now that you have seen what rules to apply—itself an exercise of judgment).

Treating customers well on the telephone is hard.[2] You have to be helpful and pleasant without being strung along, and without giving them what they want however unreasonable that may be. And the customer must end up happy. Some people are very good at it, even though they follow no rules. Most people aren't. They have to be given rules about what to say and when to say it, when to refer the complainant to the manager, when to agree, when not. So the first stage of the task gets reduced to something almost anyone can do with low failure rates.

Call center protocols require that the first responses to a new call be strictly rule based. The operative must do exactly what the manual says. No discretion, no thinking what might be best here. To do this well, you have to be conformist, to be willing to stick to the rules. Sometimes the first-stage strategy doesn't work. As the call progresses, there are rules—still rules— to tell you that you ought now to pass the caller on to another stage, because the rules to which you work are not getting there. Someone has to think about the problem.

If the call has to go to the next stage, the next operative has to decide what is going on here. Is the caller just bewildered or scared—can't understand what she is meant to do about the unpaid bill? Can't pay/won't pay? Trying it on? This stage is not simply rules based—you have to elicit what the problem really is, what kind of person you are talking to, and knowing that may not be easy, because she is muddled herself, or trying to deceive you. The manual does give you some ideas—don't think that it is only men who lie; swearing is unacceptable, but it may not show anything more than impotence. And it has some rules at the end. If she is lying, pass her on to the debt collectors; if she has temporary money problems, to the staged payments people. Or maybe you end up with the caller just paying there and then. But it is up to you how you get to where. You have to think and use your discretion. You have to decide what the next stage is. For that, you have to be, among other things, sympathetic and imaginative.

If the next stage is the debt collector, back to rules. The caller is just told to pay or else; or to pay it off over six months or. . . . To do this, you have to be tough and unsympathetic.

The lesson we get from this is that following the rules at the first stage requires the minimum of skills, experience, and personal qualities—to be able to read, to have used screen-based menus, and able and willing to conform. However able you may be generally, you don't need anything else for this purpose, and to have more than that may make you over qualified. The exercise of discretion and judgment at the second stage requires a variety of skills, experience, and personal qualities. And at the third, you need yet another set of character traits. You have to stick to the rule that they are going to pay, but you can choose a variety of approaches for getting there.

You use rules for stage one for two reasons. One is that, in very many cases, the rules get you there without difficulty. Thinking about the problem outside the rules is redundant; it adds nothing. Second, because that is so, you can employ people for stage one who are not good at exercising discretion and judgment about these problems. What they must be good at is following these particular rules. So it would be a bad idea to allow discretion at stage one because you have chosen to employ people at that stage who would not be good at it.

There is also a macro reason. There are a large number of call centers in the world. Set against the number of operatives you need to man them, those who are good at exercising the kind of judgment and discretion needed for the problem are few. The system has to be set up so that most of the decisions are made by the application of rules. If they were all made by the application of judgment, the success rate would be low, and much lower than is achieved by having rules for the first stage.

It seems a long way from call centers to deciding whether a policy will be effective. We use this example to bring out the point that deciding well is sometimes just a matter of following the rules, sometimes you have to think, and sometimes a bit of both. To get good decisions you have to decide whether in this case rules are better than discretion and judgment, and accordingly put the right sort of person in place to make the decision.

As we argue below, we say that policy making cannot, without high risk, be reduced to the operation of rules and that if you choose people who can do that, you have policy makers who are not, by temperament or training, fit to do the thinking about effectiveness that we advocate—to work through what evidence you need about how the policy will work here. Any more than the debt collector would be good at the first stage, or the first call operator at the last.

It is a matter of fact whether decisions about evidence for effectiveness take place in a world in which the qualities you need for thinking well are scarce and there is a strong prima facie need for rules. And it is a matter of fact whether there can be rules that satisfy that need. For call centers there are. That says nothing about whether there are for effectiveness decisions.

V.B.4   WHEN YOU NEED NOT THINK (MUCH, CONSCIOUSLY)

So sometimes rules are a good idea; sometimes not. Is there a theory or at least a taxonomy that can take us beyond this banality? In particular, can we get some principled insight into how this talk of rules and judgment helps with the idea that using rules-based, nonjudgmental techniques for deciding what is good evidence will lead you astray, beyond just saying that sometimes it doesn't work, bad luck? We already have something that might promise to get some structure into this part of the argument.

Our theory tells you that "it worked somewhere" is only a starting point. To get from there to "it will work here" you will need warrant for further premises about causal roles and support factors. We have been at pains to show with, for example, the failure of the Bangladesh nutrition program, that things can go badly wrong. The simple rule "find a policy with a good RCT behind it" only gets you to "it worked somewhere." To find some factor that the RCT treatment instantiates that might play the same causal role there as here, you may have to climb up the ladder of abstraction—say from "mother" to "food procurer and dispenser," using the original description of the RCT treatment as a suggestive example, and then to climb back down again to see what that amounts to in your situation—maybe "husbands, uncles or older brothers" and "mothers-in-law."

This looks complicated. It requires judgment and discretion to decide what is the right description or how to go about figuring out the right description. That process we call deliberation. Many evidence-based policy guides seem to suggest rules like "consider only policies that have been shown to work somewhere (shown by, say, two good RCTs or a good meta-analysis of RCTs)" and "take good study results of this kind as good evidence it will work for you unless, say, your situation seems different in striking ways, or unless there is evidence that your situation is different in relevant ways, or . . ." We have argued that these rules will only lead to reliable predictions about what will happen here in your situation if the RCTs have indeed fixed on a policy that can play a causal role in your situation and if you have the right support factors to ensure it will do so. If these two assumptions are met, you can just follow the rules and expect reasonably reliable predictions.

It appears to be easily believed, particularly by laymen, that in medicine a successful experience that a treatment worked on some individuals leads easily to the claim that it can play the same causal role widely. It is not hard to see why we tend to—or would prefer to—believe these things, just as it is not hard to see why we so easily take for granted that the other ingredients in our causal cake will normally be present. We like to believe that a particular intervention identifies itself by one or only a few successes as a trump or silver bullet, meaning something that will work in a large number of circumstances, and for which the presence of the support factors is in each case very likely assured.

We have argued that the assumptions that guarantee that just following these rules is a good strategy are heroic. To be justified in assuming them true you need to imagine a benign, well-behaved world. Sometimes that may be just the world your decision problem lives in. If so—and if you have good warrant for accepting that it is so—then following these rules should make your predictions reasonably reliable. But if you just follow the rule willy-nilly, you could get the result, but if so, it is a matter of lucky accident. And the point of evidence-based policy is that you should not depend on accident. You should, rather, endeavor to provide warrant for your predictions, and where you see you cannot provide warrant for them all, you should proceed with caution.

But can that be right? Do you really have to deliberate consciously and extensively every time you have to decide on effectiveness? Just as the RCT rules can paralyze action by prescribing that you follow evidence that often isn't, or can't be, there—there are no RCTs or you could not do one—are we now paralyzing action by requiring exhaustive analysis in every case? Aren't there many cases where, to use the terminology of lucky accident, you can assume that luck is on your side? There may be several cases in which behaving as though you are indeed in that more benign world will be sensible and safe.

First, you are confident about the intervention because there are a lot of studies or trials or pilots that show success, and have taken place in schools that really look like yours. The purist following our line of argument would say rightly that the phrase "like yours" does not face up to what "like" means, and it can only mean "in the relevant respects" and that must be in relation to the presumed causal role and support factors. And at once we are back in our theoretical structure, which mandates that you deliberate.

If you think it is not worth deliberating, you are perhaps in the position of the nurse who has been trained some time ago to use this and that diagnostic clue, but now has forgotten what they are, and has just become good at automatically seeing what is going on without being, or being able to be, explicit. Or you did, years ago, see that your restaurant formula works in prosperous medium-size towns in southern England with not much competition but a well off population of retired people. As time goes on, this reduces to the rule of thumb, "market towns"; and if asked, you cannot remember the extended analysis. Even later, you just know that it will work in York because it worked in Winchester, without even recalling that it is because they are both market towns. Even if this is a good way of working, you must never forget that the lessons of the theory can come back to bite you. You really should have wondered how the O-ring in the Challenger would work when it was very cold, not just assume that today was just like any other.

Second, there may be lots of studies that show it works all over the place, in almost every kind of school, not just ones like yours. This is not as likely as the first, but great if you can get it. In this case, though, you are still making a bet, and you should be aware of it.

Third, you may think that it is just obvious what to do because you have a large amount of experience, some theory, or just convincing stories, about how things work. Just as it may be absurd to require an RCT to confirm what is obvious, so it may be absurd to require deliberation.

Fourth, you may just follow the rule "mimic what good practitioners do." If you are designing a robot to paint a car well, you do not minutely analyze how it should be painted. You build a robot that follows the movements of someone who paints a car well.

Fifth, you may RCT or pilot the intervention in your school. If it works, forget why. That can be a good bet. But do recall that whether it is or not depends on what differences there will be between the pilot and full roll out.

V.B.5 WHEN RULES ARE TOXIC

Our case studies and analysis suggest the following taxonomy to clarify how and when rules and judgment can be expected to operate. Consider four possibilities:

1. You can write a good rule book, and so you don't have to rely on judgment. That is the case of the operating manual for the machine, and stage one of

the call center process. This is particularly good when, as matter of fact, the exercise of judgment—fixing the machine without the manual—would often produce a bad result. Often, using your initiative, intelligence, judgment is risky. Just do what the book says because it is a good book, better than you.

2. You can't write a good rule book. Real life problems as they present themselves in actual contexts are too heterogeneous for ex ante comprehensive rules. Maybe that is just because of our incomprehension—maybe God knows how things work and could write a manual for this machine. But the operative is bright and experienced, and we can entrust the decision to her judgment.

3. You can't write a rule book, and the operative does not have good judgment. Both following the rules and allowing discretion are dangerous.

4. You can write a rule book and the operative has good judgment. You are spoilt for choice. Economy suggests, use rules.

To tell people that they have to follow your rules for assessing evidence for effectiveness requires that you think that the rules will produce a better result than allowing them to think. This requires some combination of lack of confidence in their ability to think, and high confidence in the general applicability of the rules. You have to believe some version of 1.

We think that the injunction, "find a policy backed by a good RCT (or even better, a number of good RCTs) and implement it faithfully" does not constitute a good rule, above all because it ignores relevance. We also suspect that nobody can write a good rule for predicting effectiveness—hard social problems are inescapably open-ended and contextual. But that is not enough for you to decide to allow discretion. For that, you have to have enough confidence that the operatives to whom you will delegate have good judgment. This, possibility 2, is what you need to assume for hard local decisions.

V.B.6 SHOPPING FOR SOLUTIONS

The last section approached the problem of choosing between rules and discretion from the point of view of the center—the authority that is concerned that its agents make good decisions about policies. We analyzed two paradigm strategies for delegation—to give them free rein and to have rules to tell them what to do. We showed that according to the facts about how good a rule book you can write, and how good the agent is at exercising discretion, you should choose one strategy or the other. Or, of course, somewhere in between—do what you think best, subject to the constraint of following rules, which may vary from very loose to very tight. Neither strategy is unequivocally better than the other. A saw is not better than a hammer. It depends on the context. Thinking is not second best to following the rules. Nor vice versa.

Another way of approaching the same problem is from the standpoint of the agent who has to decide what to do. You have a social problem that you want to solve or at least make better. You want to go out and get a good solution as you might go to a store to see what is on offer. In the United States, where there is a large commercial market offering packages to help with everything from reading ability to bad behavior, that is not far from the truth. Institutions like the Cochrane or Campbell Collaborations and the What Works Clearing House can be thought of as warehouses with shelves full of policies. You can classify such warehouses and how they work for the customer according to the roles of the three main players. We use polarized alternatives.

1. What tests does a product have to pass before the *buyers* for the warehouse decide to put it on the shelves?
   a. It has very good studies to show that it worked somewhere. One of the policies worked in Tanzania.
   b. It worked in places similar to where the warehouse's customers operate: in US inner cities.
2. How can the *sales staff* help you?
   a. They just take your order for product 45/s397 and take your payment.
   b. They tell you that the best product for you will be 45/s397.
3. How good is the *customer* at thinking about her needs?
   a. Ignorant. Needs a lot of help from rules or from advice.
   b. Very expert. Understands the problem well and understands, or can get to understand, the pros and cons for her of the available products.

The worst case is all the (a) answers. The ignorant customer decides (somehow) on a product the only known characteristic of which is that it worked somewhere, and the purchase is processed. That is a very bad basis for making a decision about effectiveness. There is no thinking. Just follow the rule.

If you replace 1(a) with 1(b), things are a little better. At least you are choosing from shelves of products that have been bought with an eye to people like you. There are no washing machines for sale that work only with Tanzanian plugs. How much better can vary a lot. Maybe the buyers are rightly confident that their US customers are all much the same. Maybe that assumption is heroic. And this small variation marks the introduction of (a little) thinking. Someone, in this case the buyer not the customer, has started to wonder about which policies play causal roles that travel well and what kinds of support factors are widespread among their customers.

The best combination of the members of the list is 1(b), 2(b), and 3(b). The bright customer thinks with the helpful floor staff which of the products that have worked somewhere for customers like her is best. A lot of thinking. The evidence that it has worked somewhere is swamped in importance by all the evidence you need or would like to have about the specification of your problem, how each product works, and so on. The rule "choose a policy that is backed by an RCT" has become a constraint.

Other combinations require various other degrees of thinking by one or more of the actors. One possibility not on the list is where the buyer, the floor staff, and the customer sit down to think what tailor-made (i.e., not trialed in that exact form anywhere) solution would be best. That is the purest form of thinking, where the fact that this worked there will be no more than a starting point. But the end point may also be about whether it works here. It is likely that when the thinking has stopped, if the new policy has never been tried out anywhere, then you should trial it. Even that, though, will not guarantee that it will succeed when scaled up and implemented outside trial circumstances and in a situation that might have changed since the trial.

Even better is a three-way interaction involving scientists who design and carry out studies and who devise, develop, and test theory in partnership with the policy customer and alongside the warehouse buyer who evaluates the trustworthiness of evidence and stocks the best results. Together this team may not only produce better effectiveness predictions but also better answers to many of the other questions that good policy making involves, from "Have we settled on objectives we really want?" to "Is it cost effective?" to "Is it morally acceptable to our population?"

CONCLUSION

The centerpiece of this book has been that if you are to bet that a policy will work for you where you are, you must find the evidence relevant to that decision, and relevant means to do with the causal role that your policy will play in making a contribution to the effect that you want, and with the support factors that it will need in order to play that role.

That is about evidence for effectiveness. It is only about effectiveness. That, and that alone, is what our recommendation is about. In I.A we emphasized that effectiveness and evidence for it are only one of the many factors that enter into policy decisions. In the figure that we used there, Figure I.1, it is no more than the circle in the top right corner.

To see the importance of recognizing this limitation, consider where you are when you have done the best job you can to collect the facts needed to predict whether your policy will be effective. In terms of the Intergovernmental Panel on Climate Change categories (see section I.A.2), your confidence in the trustworthiness of that evidence and its relevance to your effectiveness prediction will range from "Very High Confidence" to "Very Low Confidence," and anywhere in between. And, as we have stressed, your confidence in the prediction can be no greater than your confidence, all told, in the body of facts that support it.

What this book has done is to tell you how to think about what facts will be relevant in order to collect the right evidence. That is what the metaphors of horizontal and vertical search, and the four strategies in III, are for.

We have said very little about trustworthiness, about how, when you have worked out what facts will be relevant, you set about validating them. More important here, we say nothing about what you do when you have done your best and have to decide what to do in light of (typically) less than perfect evidence of effectiveness. We do not say how much effectiveness matters.

What you do will rarely depend solely on your confidence that the policy will be effective. The multiple and multifarious other factors in the circles in Figure I.1 that we have not discussed will matter too. Even if, in the limiting case, you have proof-like evidence for the effectiveness of the policy, you may decide not to adopt it because of money or politics. Even if there is zero evidence of effectiveness, you may adopt it because there is a strong requirement to do something to reduce public anxiety.

In the more likely territory between these two extremes, let us say in the middling case where effectiveness is no more than likely, what will determine the decision will be considerations other than that probability, such as what are the consequences if it goes wrong, how much it matters to get a good result, and other matters to do with risk and attitude to risk. Britain's decision to support Poland in 1939 was not just to do with the effectiveness of that policy. It also depended on the idea that you should keep your promises. In an Olympic sailing race, if you think that a silver medal is just for losers, you may stop shadowing the leading boat and go off to where the wind might be better, not because the odds are good that it will be effective, but because it is your only chance. So buying a lottery ticket can be a good idea if it is the only way of transforming your life, even though the odds are provably bad that the purchase will be effective.

It follows that protocols that include cut off points—do it if it scores more than 60% probability of effectiveness—are mistaken not only because it is very unlikely that probabilities can be quantified in that way (which is why we use the IPCC phraseology of levels of confidence), but because the decision cannot be made to depend solely on any measure of effectiveness, however sophisticated. Similarly, a cut-off point that is a constraint—it must score more than 60%—will exclude policies that you should have bet on despite their low effectiveness score. If such rules are to be used, it must be recognized that they are a delegation strategy, justifiable only if the operatives are not to be trusted with the difficult task of handling the full variety of factors over the full range.

It is plain that the lower the degree of confidence, the more you should think about what would be the consequences of failure, and what you would then have to do. If a policy has low likelihood of success, it may nevertheless be worth a try, not for the reasons in the sailing example, but because it is cheap and failure doesn't matter. There are a wide range of techniques such as contingency planning and risk assessment that help with this.

But it would take another book, which we cannot write, to deal systematically with how you should take into account all the circles, all the incommensurable and heterogeneous factors that legitimately enter into intelligent and responsible decisions. We have dealt here with effectiveness, but we do not say that effectiveness is all you have to consider. We are not introducing yet another apparently comprehensive technique for cutting through the complexities of decision making. We have looked at no more than one, important, corner of the decision-making process, where we think that contemporary emphasis on trustworthiness over relevance has led us astray, and we hope to have shown how you can set about seeing what evidence you will need if you are to choose effective policies. Whatever else may be needed, that must be worth having.

Representing Causal Processes

We use sets of causal cakes to represent the causes that operate in a given situation to produce a specific outcome, to show how these break down into separate teams of support factors, and to lay out what the necessary members of each team are. This is one way of representing the causal processes by which an effect is produced. But it is only one way. It pictures certain aspects of the process but not others. Other methods of representation focus on different aspects. Here we review some of these other methods and outline what they can and cannot do.

Begin with a simple, familiar *linear chain model*, as in figure App I.1. Unlike the cakes representation, this model pictures steps in between the salient cause and the effect, as they follow one after another. This can be very helpful information, especially when you need to worry about possible breakdowns somewhere in the middle. But it lacks information available from the cakes representation. It pictures only one cake, not all the separate ones that contribute; and it pictures only one salient factor at each step, rather than the whole support team necessary at each step for the next to be produced. It also supposes a linear structure, without, for example, feedback loops. This is sometimes called a "domino" model of causation, as in figure App I.2.

Loop models are nonlinear. They can represent feedback loops, where the operation of a factor can enhance—or inhibit—the very same factor at some later time. Figure III.5 contains a causal loop model (by David Lane) from the UK 2011 Munro Review of Child Protection; figure App I.3, a different model by the same investigator to study the relations between arrivals in the accident and emergency section of a hospital and the occupancy of beds in the hospital wards. These also differ from the simple chain models in that more than one cause can be pictured feeding into the same effect, as in figure App I.3, where emergency admission rates, bed capacity,

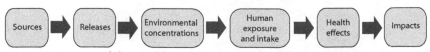

Figure App I.1: A causal chain model

Figure App I.2: The "domino" model of causation

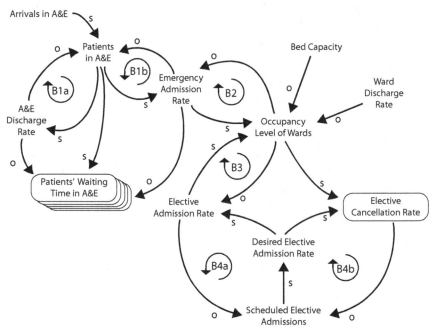

Figure App I.3: What affects waiting times in an accident and emergency (A & E) department? From Lane, Monefeldt, and Rosenhead 2000: 521.

and ward discharge rates all affect the occupancy levels of wards. What cannot be made clear in this kind of representation is how the different causes break into teams. You can't tell by looking which causes must operate together to get a contribution from them at all and which are in totally different teams, each of which is sufficient to produce a contribution. This is a drawback over the cakes method of representation.

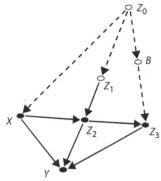

Figure App I.4: Example of a directed acyclic graph (or DAG) typical of Bayes Nets methods of causal inference. From Pearl 2009: 67.

Directed acyclic graphs are commonly associated with the Bayes Nets methods of causal inference mentioned in I.B.5.3. "Acyclic" means they don't have loops. They look like figure App I.4, which is due to Judea Pearl (2009: 67), who is one of the central developers of these methods. As with simple chain models and loop models, these lay out one step after another of various causal processes involved and they give information about different causes leading into the same effect. In cases where it is clear what this means, information about the relative size of contributions from different causes can be added by putting numbers alongside the various arrows. This is typically done in the path diagrams that used to be popular in sociology. As with loop diagrams, and unlike the cake representation, these do not tell you which factors must support each other to make a complete team that is sufficient for a contribution.

None of the methods so far show the relative size of contributions from different teams nor exactly how the members of the same team fit together to produce a contribution. For instance, in the contribution that the gravitational attraction of an object of mass M makes to the total force on an object of mass m—GMm/r^2—the masses multiply, so that the contribution increases as each gets bigger; the value of the distance is squared; and the contribution due to gravity gets smaller as the distance gets larger. Nor do they represent how different contributions combine, for instance by summing, or, as with forces in classical mechanics, by vector addition. You can get all that, plus sequencing, if you use sets of equations, as is typical in time series models in econometrics. Consider, for instance, the Solow growth model for an economy, as presented by a contemporary economist (Klemp 2011: 3–4):

> The Solow model describes a closed economy without government spending in the long run.
> [...] We formulate a Solow model in continuous time with time-varying savings rate, $s(t)$, and
> population growth rate, $n(t)$ ...

Total output, Y (t) is given by the Cobb-Douglas production function

$$(1) \ Y(t) = K(t)^{\lambda} (A(t)L(t))^{\mu}, \lambda, \mu \in (0,1), Y(t), K(t), L(t) > 0$$

where $K(t)$ is aggregate capital input, $L(t)$ is the total labour input and $A(t)$ is the labour-augmenting technological progress. The stock of technology grows with the constant rate g, i.e.

$$(2) \ \dot{A}(t) = gA(t)$$

The fundamental law of motion describes the evolution of capital in the equilibrium by

$$(3) \ \dot{K}(t) = s(t)Y(t) - \delta K(t), \delta \in (0,1)$$

where $s(t)$ is the fraction of output that goes to savings and thus investment, since the economy is closed. The parameter δ is the depreciation rate of capital.

The total labour input grows with the rate $n(t)$

$$(4) \ \dot{L}(t) = n(t)L(t)$$

... We now turn to specify the evolution of the savings rate and the population growth rate. The savings rate is given by the first-order linear ordinary differential equation

$$(5) \ \dot{s}(t) = \bar{s} - (1 - \rho_s)s(t), \bar{s} > 0, \rho_s \in (0,1)$$

This equation says that the savings rate will converge to its long-run equilibrium value ...

In this model you see how the savings and population growth rates change through time and how this affects the three factors that multiply together in the Cobb Douglas function to fix total output. This kind of model is about as complete in its representational capacity as it can get. But it is not generally available, and this is not due only to human ignorance. Causal relations among many factors may well not have this kind of precise functional form. Indeed, many causal factors may not themselves be precise measurable quantities to begin with. So this kind of representation may simply not be available.

We present this brief survey to point out that different methods of representation are good for representing different aspects of how causes manage to produce their effects. In this book, we rely primarily on causal cakes. We do so because cakes and their ingredients highlight aspects that we see too frequently overlooked in advice about how to use evidence to predict effectiveness. In general, representations should be chosen to fit the purposes in view; and different representations can be used together to give a fuller picture. But it must always be remembered that what they picture, singly or in cohort, may well not be all that matters.

APPENDIX II

The Munro Review

We reproduce below the text that follows the causal loop diagram, Figure III.5 in this book, found in Appendix A of the Munro Review (Munro 2011: 136–38). It provides the story underlying the diagram.

1. The increase in rules and guidance governing child and family social work activity over the past two decades has had a number of unintended consequences on the health of their profession and outcomes for vulnerable children and young people. Some are illustrated in this "causal loop diagram."

2. The quality of the outcomes for children and young people delivered by child protection services is heavily influenced by three factors. First, the wide variety of needs that children and young people have; the more variety, the harder it is to meet those needs. Second, professionals can only work within the scope that they are allowed for applying their professional expertise. If that scope is increased, alongside an investment in building social workers' capabilities, then it is likely that outcomes for children will improve. Third, outcomes are also improved when professionals establish and maintain high quality relationships with children, young people and their families.

3. Increasing prescription for the ways in which child and family social workers respond to children and families' needs has had a number of ripple effects in the system. These have primarily manifested themselves as unintended consequences on the ability of children's social care to protect children and young people and feedback effects (see below for definition) forming damaging "vicious circles."

4. For example, too much prescription of practice, which diminishes professional responsibility for judgments and decisions, has an unintended

consequence of reducing the job satisfaction, self-esteem and sense of personal responsibility experienced by child protection workers. This leads to the further unintended consequence of increasing amounts of time taken off absent or sick. In fact, this goes on to create a reinforcing loop, R1 (see below for definition): those still at work have to take on larger caseloads and in turn have less time to build relationships with children and families; in time, this reduces the quality of the outcomes for children and young people, which further reduces the sense of job satisfaction.

5. Another unintended consequence of prescription is that dissatisfaction with the role causes high staff turnover. Again, this creates larger caseloads and reduced contact time with children, young people and families, so another vicious circle is created, R2.

6. Two other influences are illustrated, each exacerbating the ripple effects. Too much prescription reduces scope for professionals to respond appropriately to each individual case and, though it takes longer for the effect to play out, this reduces the quality of outcomes for children and families. In addition, the large amounts of time social workers are forced to spend on Integrated Children's System (ICS), reduces the time they can spend directly engaging with children, young people and families. Both of these can be seen as unintended consequences of burdensome rules and guidance. However, they also strengthen the two feedback effects (reduced job satisfaction due to increased caseloads as a result of absence and high turnover), making these loops even more damaging.

7. Although only a few "ripple effects" are illustrated here, they are indicative of a range of unintended consequences resulting from an overly-prescriptive approach to child and family social work. This collection of reinforcing loops has restricted the capabilities of the profession, increasingly reducing its effectiveness.

APPENDIX III

CCTV and Car Theft

What follows is taken from Pawson and Tilley (1997: 78–81) by kind permission of SAGE Publications Ltd. It is reproduced in its entirety here, not because it maps perfectly onto our analysis and terminology (in particular, in its use of the term "mechanism"), but because it illustrates admirably one of our major lessons—that if you are thinking about what may be relevant to your effectiveness prediction, the list will be long and heterogeneous.

We choose as our example of realist theory in action a programming area which is seemingly mundane and mechanical. We want to look at car parks. More specifically, we wish to examine the problem of car park crime and attempts to reduce it through the installation of closed-circuit television (CCTV). Such programs, in fact, share a key characteristic with all social initiatives. There is nothing about police patrols which intrinsically reduces fear of crime. There is nothing about education programs which intrinsically reduces offender reconviction. So too, there is nothing about CCTV in car parks which intrinsically inhibits car crime. Whilst *it* may appear to offer a technical solution, CCTV certainly does not create a physical barrier making cars impenetrable. A moment's thought has us realize, therefore, that the cameras must work by instigating a chain of reasoning and reaction. Realist evaluation is all about turning this moment's thought into a comprehensive theory of the mechanisms through which CCTV may enter the potential criminal's mind, and the contexts needed if these powers are to be realized. We begin with mechanisms.

(a) *The "caught in the act" mechanism.* CCTV could reduce car crime by making it more likely that *present offenders* will be observed on screen, detected instantly and then arrested, removed, punished and deterred.

(b) *The "you've been framed" mechanism*. CCTV could reduce car crime be deterring *potential offenders* who will not wish to risk investigation, apprehension and conviction by the evidence captured on videotape.

(c) *The "nosy parker" mechanism*. The presence of CCTV may lead to increases in usage of car parks, because drivers feel less at risk of victimization. Increased usage could then enhance natural surveillance which may deter potential offenders, who feel they are at increased risk of apprehension in the course of criminal behavior.

(d) *The "effective deployment" mechanism*. CCTV may facilitate the effective deployment of security staff or police officers towards areas where suspicious behaviour is occurring. They then act as a visible presence which might deter potential offenders. They may also apprehend actual offenders red-handed and disable their criminal behaviour.

(e) *The "publicity" mechanism*. CCTV, and signs indicating that it is in operation, could symbolize efforts to take crime seriously and to reduce it. The potential offender may be led to avoid the increased risk they believe to be associated with committing car crimes in car parks and so be deterred.

(f) *The "time for crime" mechanism*. Those car crimes which can be completed in a very short space of time may decline less than those which take more time, as offenders calculate the time taken for police or security officers to come or the probability that panning cameras will focus in on them.

(g) *The "memory jogging" mechanism*. CCTV and notices indicating that it is in operation may remind drivers that their cars are vulnerable, and they may thereby be prompted to take greater care to lock them, to operate any security devices, and to remove easily stolen items from view.

(h) *The "appeal to the cautious" mechanism*. It might be that cautious drivers, who are sensitive to the possibility that their cars may be vulnerable and are habitual users of various security devices, use and fill the car parks that have CCTV and thereby drive out those who are more careless, whose vulnerable cars are stolen from elsewhere.

It is clearly possible that more than one of these mechanisms for change may operate simultaneously. Which (if any) mechanisms are fired turns on the context in which CCTV is installed, and this may vary widely. Consider the following:

(i) *The "criminal clustering" context*. A given rate of car crime may result from widely differing prevalences of offending. For example if there are 1,000 incidents per annum, this may be by anything from a single (very busy) offender to as many as 1,000 offenders, or still more if they operate in groups. A mechanism leading to disablement of the offender (as in (a) above) holds potential promise according to the offender-offence ratio.

(ii) *The "style of usage" context.* A long stay car park may have an enormous influx of vehicles between eight and eight-thirty in the morning when it becomes full up. It may then empty between five and six in the evening. If the dominant CCTV fired mechanism turns out to be increased confidence and usage (and in (h) or (c) above) then this will have little impact because the pattern of usage is already high with little movement, dictated by working hours not fear of crime. If, however, the car park is little used, but has a very high per user car crime rate, then the increased usage mechanism may lead to an overall increase in numbers of crime a decreased rate per use.

(iii) *The "lie of the land" context.* Cars parked in the CCTV blind spots in car parks will be more vulnerable if the mechanism is increased chances of apprehension through evidence on videotape (as in (b) above), but not if it is through changed attributes or security behaviour of customers (as in (g) or (h) above).

(iv) *The "alternative targets" context.* The local patterns of motivation of offenders, together with the availability of alternative targets of car crime, furnish aspects of the wider context for displacement to car crimes elsewhere, whatever crime reduction mechanisms may be fired by CCTV in the specific context of a given car park.

(v) *The "resources" context.* In an isolated car park with no security presence and the police at some distance away, the deployment of security staff or police as a mobile and flexible resource to deter car crime (as in (d) above) is not possible.

(vi) *The "surveillance culture" context.* As the usage of CCTV surveillance spreads through all walks of life and features in extensive media portrayal of "modern policing," the efficacy of the publicity given to CCTV in car parks (as in (e) above) may be enhanced or muted, according to the overall reputation of such surveillance.

We do not pretend that this listing of potential contexts and mechanisms is mutually exclusive or totally inclusive. What we trust it reveals instantly, however, is that a bit of lateral thinking in the realm of hypothesis making requires that we trudge well off the beaten tracks in the search for supporting empirical evidence. Despite the somewhat ad hoc character of our lists (there being no existing sociology of the car park), we nevertheless thus make the strong claim that an investigation framed around these ideas will yield far more of worth than one driven by the quasi-experimental starting point of comparing car crime rates before and after CCTV installation. These hypotheses frame the requisite data and research strategies, and thus call upon a range of evidence entirely different from the standard comparisons. A series of studies would be required to sift, sort and adjudicate which of the various mechanism/context permutations was active, a task we can summarize with the following highly abbreviated list of investigative tacks.

1. As well as seeking for reductions in crime rate, following CCTV installation, it would be important to check on *convictions* attributable to CCTV, for this would reveal whether direct detection or taped evidence (as in (a) and (b) above) were actually capable of generating the outcome. Further evidence on these detection mechanisms could be compiled by actually inspecting the *technical capabilities* of systems in respect of whether their resolution power could identify individuals or in respect of how quickly they were capable of homing in to an offence. Tilley [(1993)] reports on highly limited performance in respect of both conviction and technique, inclining him to the belief that the remaining, indirect, risk perception mechanisms are more crucial.

2. Before-and-after data, again not just on changing rate but on changes in *type* of crime and of *criminal opportunities*, may be a crucial next step but, as far as we are aware, one that has not been utilized with respect to these programs. A survey ascertaining changes in number of cars left locked and in the extent to which attractive goods were left on display would allow some test of the "appeal to the cautious" and "memory jogging" mechanisms (h) and (g). This could be complemented with data on the changing pattern of thefts from cars, including the sorts of items stolen, and where they were in the car, to test the "time for crime" mechanism (f). Without the prior theory, it is by no means obvious that actually examining unmolested parked cars would constitute an important part of the evaluation process.

3. Another important body of evidence would concern the *location* within the car park of crimes committed. If these had some spatial concentration, it would demonstrate that the potential thief had a (perhaps sophisticated) understanding of camera angles, panning times, blind spots, escape routes, response times etc. Thinking through the local geography of the outcomes would allow us to test aspects of the "lie of the land" context (iii) as well as features of the aforementioned mechanisms (b), (d), (f), (g). These would in turn produce good process-evaluation data for the refinement of CCTV installations.

4. Data on the *temporal* patterning of crime, cross-referenced perhaps to information on the amount of *capacity* in use at any time, would be the obvious material to test the influence of the "style of usage" context (ii). As well as informing us on whether the potential offender feared natural surveillance more or less than CCTV surveillance, a more elaborate investigation of outcomes across a range of types of car parks (long stay, short stay,

commuter, rail, shopper, works etc.) will provide some evidence of the pattern of perceived risks associated with different sites, as well as intelligence on the most beneficial CCTV locations.

5. Hard evidence on the "publicity" mechanism (e) and "surveillance culture" context (vi) is probably the most difficult (and we suspect, the most important) to ascertain. A start on this could be made by pursuing some (experimental-type!) variations in the publicity attendant on the arrival of the CCTV cameras to see if the specifics of the message made a discernible difference to outcomes. A periodic reworking/refreshing of publicity could also be undertaken in order to detect whether the car crime rate over time was responsive. As with all of the risk perception mechanisms, potentially the most valuable data may well come from the potential risk takers themselves. In this respect, we hit a standard catch-22 of criminological research: the greater the success of a publicity deterrent, the greater the difficulty in the construction of a sample of the very respondents one needs (the deterred).

NOTES

CHAPTER I.A

1. We take this account from a report of the World Bank Independent Evaluation Group (World Bank 1995). It is not uncontroversial (cf. Sridhar 2008) but we propose to take it as correct in order to use it in illustration.
2. See http://ies.ed.gov/ncee/wwc/ for the US What Works Clearing House, http://www.povertyactionlab.org/ for J-PAL, and http://www.campbellcollaboration.org/ for the Campbell Collaboration.
3. See the policy guidelines available at http://www2.ed.gov/rschstat/research/pubs/rigorousevid/index.html.
4. See http://www.sign.ac.uk/guidelines/fulltext/50/index.html for the Scottish Intercollegiate Guidelines Network and http://www.cebm.net/index.aspx?o=1025 for the Oxford Centre for Evidence-Based Medicine.

CHAPTER I.B

1. Unless, of course, French could produce another valid argument in which the measurements figure and where all the other premises can be assumed with confidence.
2. Note that we claim that causes are INUS conditions. But not the converse, that all INUS conditions are causes. The terminology comes from Mackie (1965).
3. See (7) immediately following.
4. We wish to stress, as remarked in the text, that we use this simple linear form to avoid needless complications and to make the discussion easier to follow. Exactly the same lessons follow from more complicated forms, including, especially, the lesson that the RCT treatment effect is a function of the average over the values of the support factors in the RCT population.
5. For a skeptical take on this issue, see Worrall 2002, 2007.
6. See http://www.campbellcollaboration.org/what_is_a_systematic_review/index.php.
7. This argument was originally formulated by Hilary Putnam 1975: 73.
8. See, for instance, Pearl 2009: 146.
9. For more on instrumental variables, see Reiss 2005 or Angrist, Imbens, and Rubin 1996.
10. See Fennell 2007 and Cartwright 2007.

CHAPTER II.A

1. We will discuss the case of continuous variables below, where you can get more or less of the effect depending on the values of the input variables.
2. For more details, see Robinson 2006 and Hagel et al. 2006.

CHAPTER II.B

1. The detail of this part, for example, the proper names, is fictitious. This example is taken from Cartwright and Stegenga 2011 and does not reproduce what appears in the World Bank and other relevant literature.

CHAPTER III.B

1. See Klein 1999 and Mitchell, Russo, and Pennington 1989.
2. The device in this example is *LongPen*, which was subsequently commercialized success-fully by Syngrafii Corp. The account here is not from public sources and is based on the investigations Jeremy had to make at the time of his original investment in September 2008.
3. This section is based on Carvalho and White 2004.
4. Pawson and Tilley talk about "mechanisms" in this regard. We do not use this term because it has too many different meanings. Also, "mechanism" may suggest something like the inner workings of the toaster or what's under the hood of the car, or, alternatively, the causal sequence by which the policy produces the effect (which we called "how it does so" in III.B.2). Here we are, by contrast, urging you to look for a general feature that is widely shared.
5. Pawson and Tilley's use of "mechanism" and "context" does not map easily onto our ter-minology of finding the abstract feature in virtue of which the concrete policy variable works and of support factors. But that doesn't matter for the point that we use the list for, that if you are deliberating about our two questions, the list can get very long and hetero-geneous. The lists are from Pawson and Tilley 1997: 78–79. See also Appendix III.
6. Our quick exit decision trees are a close relation of Gerd Gigerenzer's "One-Reason Decision Making" and his notion of "Fast and Frugal Trees." See, for example, Gigerenzer and Gaissmaier 2011: 463 and 467.

CHAPTER IV.B

1. See Seckinelgin (2007) for concerns about how far these study results can travel.
2. This case study is a stylized account of Jeremy Hardie's experience as a director of Bras-serie Blanc PLC, a British restaurant chain.

CHAPTER IV.C

1. See *Identifying and Implementing Educational Practices Supported by Rigorous Evidence: A User Friendly Guide* at the following address: http://www2.ed.gov/rschstat/research/pubs/rigorousevid/guide_pg6.html.
2. See the reference given above in note 2 of chapter 1A.
3. The program has to pass *at least* these tests. This is a summary.

CHAPTER IV.D

1. The GLA guidelines say that "it is now established that programmes that are delivered with what is called 'fidelity'—meaning they are implemented as intended by the pro-gramme designers—achieve the best results" (2010: 9).
2. They also, of course, may have a commercial motive.
3. See USDE 2003: 14, for instance.
4. As reported in *The Independent*, London, Thursday July 28, 2011, from *Key conclusions from the meeting of scientific experts*, DEFRA, April 4, 2011.
5. Which is what the GLA says: "do not change the core elements . . . without good evidence that changes are needed" (GLA 2010: 18).

6. The demand for two RCTs also nods toward breadth. If the result obtains in two different settings, then it isn't due to totally peculiar local circumstances. The two motives pull in opposite directions. For the first, to help guard against the result from an RCT being one of those entirely possible but highly improbable happenings, the circumstances of the second RCT should be just like the first; to ensure the result is not due to very special local conditions, the circumstances should be different.

7. Fight for Peace is a UK-based charity that operates to overcome division and violence among young people, at present in London and Rio de Janeiro. See Sampson 2009; Madgin 2008; and FOC 2006.

8. Private conversation with Luke Dowdney, founder of Fight for Peace.

9. Private conversation with Luke Dowdney.

10. CDFIs are not-for-profit entities with funds from the state or foundations set up to provide lending and investment outside the normal private sector system.

CHAPTER V.B

1. Passim and in Gigerenzer and Gaissmaier 2011, who quote Serwe and Frings 2006, and Scheibehenne and Bröder 2007.

2. For a generic account of how personal profiling can be used to fit people to jobs, see http://www.thomasinternational.net/manage/Benchmarking.aspx.

REFERENCES

Allen MP, G. (2011). *Early Intervention: The Next Steps*. An Independent Report to Her Majesty's Government. London: Her Majesty's Government.

Angrist, J., Imbens, G., and Rubin, D. (1996). "Identification of Causal Effects Using Instrumental Variables," *Journal of the American Statistical Association*, 91: 444–55.

APA (2002). "Criteria for Evaluating Treatment Guidelines," *American Psychologist*, 57: 1052–59.

Bahor, T., et al. (2010). *Drug Policy and the Public Good*. New York: Oxford University Press.

Balshem, H., et al. (2011). "GRADE Guidelines: 3. Rating the Quality of Evidence," *Journal of Clinical Epidemiology*, 64: 401–06.

Bohrnstedt, G., and Stecher, B., eds. (2002). *What We have Learned about Class Size Reduction in California*. Sacramento: California Department of Education.

Bourne, F., et al. (2007). *Bovine TB: The Scientific Evidence*. London: Department of Environment, Food and Rural Affairs.

Cartwright, N. (2007). *Hunting Causes and Using Them: Approaches in Philosophy and Economics*. Cambridge: Cambridge University Press.

Cartwright, N., and Stegenga, J. (2011). "A Theory of Evidence for Evidenced-Based Policy," in W. Twining, P. Dawid, and D. Vasilaki (eds.), *Evidence, Inference and Enquiry*. New York: Oxford University Press.

Carvalho, S., and White, H. (2004). "Theory-Based Evaluation: The Case of Social Funds," *American Journal of Evaluation*, 25: 141–60.

Chintu, C., et al. (2004). "Co-trimoxazole as Prophylaxis against Opportunistic Infections in HIV-infected Zambian Children (CHAP): A Double-blind Randomised Placebo controlled Trial," *The Lancet*, 364: 1865–71.

Cooper, H., Robinson, J. C., and Patall, E. A. (2006). "Does Homework Improve Academic Achievement? A Synthesis of Research, 1987–2004," *Review of Educational Research*, 76: 1–62.

Crofts, F. W. (2001). *Death on the Way*. Thirsk: House of Stratus.

Davies, P. (2005). "Evidence-Based Policy at the Cabinet Office," presentation given at the *Impact and Insight Seminar*, Overseas Development Institute, London, October 17, 2005. http://www.odi.org.uk/rapid/events/impact_insight/presentation_1/davies.html.

EFF (2005). *Street (UK): Learning from Community Finance*. London: Esmée Fairbairn Foundation.

Fennell, D. (2007). "Why Functional Form Matters: Revealing the Structure in Structural Models in Econometrics," *Philosophy of Science* (Supplement), 74: 1033–45.

FOC (2006). *Avaliação do Projeto Luta Pela Paz-Maré-Rio de Janeiro*. Rio de Janeiro: Fundação Oswaldo Cruz.

Galison, P. (2004). "Mirror Symmetry: Persons, Values, and Objects," in N. Wise (ed.), *Growing Explanations: Historical Perspectives on Recent Science*. Durham, NC: Duke University Press.

Gigerenzer, G., and Gaissmaier, W. (2011). "Heuristic Decision Making," *Annual Review of Psychology*, 62: 451–82.

GLA (2010). *Standards of Evidence the Greater London Authority*. Oracle Project. London: Greater London Authority.

Hagel, B., et al. (2006). "Arguments against Helmet Legislation are Flawed," *British Medical Journal*, 332: 725–76.

Heckman, J., and Vytlacil, E. (2007). "Econometric Evaluation of Social Programs," parts I and II, in J. Heckman and E. Leamer (eds.), *Handbook of Econometrics*, Vol. 6B. Amsterdam: Elsevier.

Hendry, D., and Mizon, G. (2011). "What Needs Rethinking in Macroeconomics?" *Global Policy*, 2: 176–83.

IPCC (2006). *Guidance Notes for Lead Authors of the IPCC Fourth Assessment Report on Addressing Uncertainties*. Geneva: Intergovernmental Panel on Climate Change.

Klein, G. (1999). *Sources of Power: How People Make Decisions*. Cambridge, MA: MIT Press.

Klemp, M. (2011). "Time-Series Analysis of the Solow Growth Model," University of Copenhagen, mimeo.

Lane, D., Monefeldt, C., and Rosenhead, J. (2000). " Looking in the Wrong Place for Healthcare Improvements: A System Dynamics Study of an Accident and Emergency Department," *Journal of the Operational Research Society*, 51: 518–31.

Leamer, E. (2010). "Tantalus on the Road to Asymptotia," *Journal of Economic Perspectives*, 24: 31–46.

Lucas, R. (1976). "Econometric Policy Evaluation: A Critique," in K. Brunner and A. Meltzer (eds.), *The Phillips Curve and Labor Markets*. Carnegie-Rochester Conference Series on Public Policy, Vol. 1. Amsterdam: North Holland.

Ludwig, J., et al. (2008). "What Can We Learn about Neighborhood Effects from the Moving to Opportunity Experiment?" *American Journal of Sociology*, 114: 144–88.

Mackie, J. L. (1965). "Causes and Conditions," *American Philosophical Quarterly*, 2: 245–64.

Madgin, R. (2008). *Report of the Implementation of Fight for Peace in East London 2007–08*. London: University of East London, Center for Institutional Studies.

Meinert, C. (1995). "The Inclusion of Women in Clinical Trials," *Science*, 269: 795–96.

MHRA (2004). *Report of the CSM Expert Working Group on the Safety of Selective Serotonin Reuptake Inhibitor Antidepressants*. London: Medicines and Healthcare Products Regulatory Agency.

Mill, J. S. [1836] (1967). "On the Definition of Political Economy and on the Method of Philosophical Investigation in That Science," in *Collected Works of John Stuart Mill*, Vol. 4. Toronto: University of Toronto Press.

———. [1843] (1850). *A System of Logic*. New York: Harper and Brothers.

Mitchell, D., Russo, E., and Pennington, N. (1989). "Back to the Future: Temporal Perspective in the Explanation of Events," *Journal of Behavioral Decision Making*, 2: 25–38.

Munro, E. (2011). *The Munro Review of Child Protection: Final Report*. London: UK Department of Education.

Pawson, R., and Tilley, N. (1997). *Realistic Evaluation*. London: SAGE Publications.

PC (1986). *Report to the President by the Presidential Commission on the Space Shuttle Challenger Disaster*. Washington, DC.

Pearl, J. (2009). *Causality: Models, Reasoning, and Inference*. 2nd ed. New York: Oxford University Press.

———. (2010). "The Foundations of Causal Inference," *Sociological Methodology*, 40: 75–149.

Putnam, H. (1975). *Mathematics, Matter and Method*. Cambridge: Cambridge University Press.

Reiss, J. (2005). "Causal Instrumental Variables and Interventions," *Philosophy of Science* (Supplement), 72: 964–76.

Risbey, J., and Kandlikar, M. (2007). "Expressions of Likelihood and Confidence in the IPCC Uncertainty Assessment Process," *Climate Change*, 85: 19–31.

Robinson, D. (2006). "No Clear Evidence from Countries that have Enforced the Wearing of Helmets," *British Medical Journal*, 332: 722–25.

Sampson, A. (2009). *The Fight for Peace Academy UK: An Independent Assessment*. London: University of East London, Center for Institutional Studies.

Scheibehenne, B., and Bröder, A. (2007). "Predicting Wimbledon 2005 Tennis Results by Mere Player Name Recognition," *International Journal of Forecasting*, 23: 415–26.

Seckinelgin, H. (2007). "Evidence-based Policy for HIV/AIDS Interventions: Questions of External Validity, or Relevance for Use," *Development and Change*, 38: 1219–34.

Serwe, S., and Frings, C. (2006). "Who will Win Wimbledon? The Recognition Heuristic and Predicting Sports Events," *Journal of Behavioral Decision Making*, 19: 321–32.

Sridhar, D. (2008). *The Battle against Hunger: Choice, Circumstance, and the World Bank*. New York: Oxford University Press.

STC (2003). *Thin in the Ground: Questioning the Evidence behind World Bank-funded Community Nutrition Projects in Bangladesh, Ethiopia and Uganda*. London: Save the Children UK.

Tilley, N. (1993). *Understanding Car Parks, Crime and CCTV*. Crime Prevention Unit Paper 42. London: Home Office.

UKDPC (2008). *Working towards Recovery: Getting Problem Drug Users into Jobs*. London: UK Drug Policy Commission.

USDE (2003). *Identifying and Implementing Educational Practices Supported by Rigorous Evidence: A User Friendly Guide*. Washington, DC: Coalition for Evidence-Based Policy. http://www2.ed.gov/rschstat/research/pubs/rigorousevid/index.html.

White, H. (2009). "Theory-based Impact Evaluation: Principles and Practice," *3ie Working Paper No. 3*. New Delhi: International Initiative for Impact Evaluation.

World Bank (1995). *Tamil Nadu and Child Nutrition: A New Assessment*. Washington, DC: World Bank.

Worrall, J. (2002). "What Evidence in Evidence-Based Medicine?" *Philosophy of Science*, 69: S316–30.

———. (2007). "Why There's No Cause to Randomize," *British Journal for the Philosophy of Science*, 58: 451–88.

INDEX

abstraction
   ladder of, 79, 84, 86–88, 91, 93, 145–46,
      148, 166
   levels of, 79, 84, 86, 148
advice guides, 135–36
Allen, Graham, 140, 143
argument, good, 5, 16, 18–19, 53, 57
argument pyramid, 16–20, 133–34

Becker, Gary, 86
BINP (Bangladesh Integrated Nutrition
   Project), 3, 80–82, 145

cakes. *See* causal cakes
Campbell Collaboration, 37, 136
causal cakes, 9, 61–74, 76, 78, 82, 84, 97,
   113
causal principles, 23–24, 26–36, 41–46,
   50–52, 54, 56, 78–80, 128
   shared, 79
causal process, 71
causal roles, 6, 43–45, 49–52, 54–55, 62, 76,
   78, 88, 113, 127, 158, 160, 172
CCTV, 109–12
control, placebo, 40
control groups, 33–34, 38, 40

decision trees, quick exit, 113–18, 162
deliberation, 158–60, 162, 166

effectiveness, 5, 7, 11, 13, 23, 53–54, 136,
   138
Effectiveness Argument, 45, 54, 57–58
effectiveness predictions, 5, 15, 22, 30, 44,
   50–51, 53–54, 123
   RCTs and, 33, 40, 56, 133
   reliable, 11, 132
efficacy, 7, 32, 41

evidence, 9, 13–15, 18–19, 21–22, 50–51,
   53–54, 136, 138
   empirical, 21
   gold-standard, 8
evidence for use, theory of, 14, 51, 61
evidence-ranking schemes, 7, 9–10, 36–37,
   121, 136, 139, 148, 158, 161

feedback loops, 107, 109
FFP (Fight for Peace), 147–48
fidelity, 144–46, 148, 150

Gigerenzer, Gerd, 162
GLA (Greater London Authority), 130,
   141–42, 163
GRADE (Grading of Recommendations
   Assessment, Development and Evalua-
   tion), 36, 138

heuristics, 10, 162
horizontal search, 61, 64–66, 69, 82 84,
   91, 100

intervention, early, 140
INUS conditions, 25, 27, 44, 63–65, 71,
   78, 160
IPCC (International Panel on Climate
   Change), 5

judgment, exercise of, 159, 163–64, 169

LongPen, 95, 99
Lucas critique, 31

magic bullet, 73, 118, 146
malnutrition, 3
masking, 34–35, 40
meta-analyses, 36

method-of-difference study, 33
Mill, John Stuart, 33, 43
model, five pillar, 147, 149
MTO (Moving To Opportunity), 47–48
Munro Review, 109

necessary conditions, 70, 72, 113–14, 150

PDUs (problem drug users), 114–16, 118
pie. *See* causal cakes
pilots, 87, 129, 167–68
policy effectiveness. *See* effectiveness
policy effectiveness predictions.
    See effectiveness predictions
policy variable, 26, 69, 72–73, 84, 109, 114
premises, 15–23
pre-mortem, 97, 99
principles
    general, 87
    lower level, 86
    See also causal principles
probabilistic dependencies, 38–39
probabilities, 37, 39, 47, 57, 118
process tracing, 38–39
pubs, 117–18

random assignment, 34–35
    See also randomization
randomization, 38, 40
    See also random assignment
randomized controlled trial. *See* RCTs
ranking schemes. *See* evidence-ranking
    schemes
RBCT (Randomized Badger Culling Trial),
    144–45
RCT Argument, 35, 38, 40, 46, 57–58, 122
RCTs (randomized controlled trial), 4, 7,
    10, 23, 28, 33–34, 38, 40, 56–58, 111,
    122–23, 126–27, 132, 140
    ideal, 34, 38

relevance, 10, 15, 32, 34, 41, 57, 112, 123,
    139–41, 158, 161, 169, 174
    evidential, 18, 22
    theory of, 15
replication, 145–46
rules, 158–59, 161–71

sample, 128
similarity, 46–49
social funds, 102, 106
social policy, 11, 27, 91–93, 99, 125–26,
    128, 160
step-by-step strategy, 20, 100–101, 107
support factors, 25, 41–42, 44–51, 54–55,
    61–65, 69, 71–72, 84, 91, 99, 158
    the distribution of, 41–42, 48

tendencies, stable, 43–44
TINP (Tamil Nadu Integrated Nutrition
    Project), 3, 81, 88
treatment effect, 34, 36, 40–41, 46–49, 123
treatment group, 33–34
trees, quick exit. *See* decision trees, quick
    exit
trustworthiness, 10, 32, 34, 38, 139,
    171–74

unintended consequences, 69
US Department of Education, 10, 12, 122,
    125, 139, 146, 163
utility, 86–87

validity
    external, 45–47, 49
    internal, 46
vertical search, 61, 79–80, 83–84, 91–92,
    103, 127

warrant, 15–19, 53
World Bank, 3, 84, 102

CPSIA information can be obtained
at www.ICGtesting.com
Printed in the USA
BVHW080757230120
570242BV00003B/19

9 780199 841622